ADVANCE PRAISE FOR

DAMNED NATIONS

"A brave, eloquent, and necessary book."

– LEWIS LAPHAM, editor, *Lapham's Quarterly*

"Samantha Nutt is scrupulously consistent with her hard-nosed, direct, in-your-face style and defiant resolve in her approach to war and the massive abuses to humanity, especially women and children. Samantha is telling us in no uncertain terms that humanitarianism starts by a 'critical reflection concerning our own actions and deeds.' And then she offers some solid proposals to consider. Well done, in a most compelling of ways."

– LGEN THE HON. ROMÉO A. DALLAIRE, (Ret'd), Senator, author of *Shake Hands With the Devil*

"Dr. Nutt movingly outlines the chilling truth about war and offers us a rare, poignant glimpse into each individual's part in the process to attainable peace. An absolute must-read for every person in the developed world, and a manual for every leader."

– CHANTAL KREVIAZUK, Juno Award–winning performer and songwriter, and activist

"This is an extraordinarily riveting book. The anecdotes are heart-wrenching; the analysis is trenchant, principled, uncompromising. I never read a book in one sitting: I read *Damned Nations* in one sitting, and I regretted that it came to an end. It's filled with emotional and intellectual power."

– STEPHEN LEWIS, former Canadian Ambassador to the United Nations, and Chair of the Board of the Stephen Lewis Foundation

"When I first met Sam, I was moved by her total and single-minded dedication to justice. She thought of people in far away places the way we think of relatives in disadvantage, and she behaved like we do at our best when we care enough to do something. I have no doubt you will be moved by her stories and her work, but I hope most of all, by her example."

– K'NAAN, Juno Award–winning performer, songwriter, poet, and activist

"What makes this book especially valuable is how Samantha Nutt weaves into personal experiences of war, a damning assessment of how governments, private corporations, indeed even NGOs, are culpable for much suffering by turning a blind eye to the consequences of the small arms trade, the rapacious search for scarce resources and commodities, the use of the military over diplomatic solutions, and the false start of so many aid and development initiatives. This book is a passionate reaction to so much of the stupidity and calumny that leads to death and destruction, and yet it incorporates insightful and cool-headed reasons as to why. An important book for our times."

> – LLOYD AXWORTHY, President, University of Winnipeg
> and former Minister of Foreign Affairs

"This is an extraordinary book. From its opening scenes, my heart was in my throat. Samantha Nutt is a genuine hero. All of us living in the comfort and affluence of industrialized countries, owe it to the rest of humanity to read this powerful book."

> – DAVID SUZUKI, co-founder, The David Suzuki Foundation,
> and Professor Emeritus, University of British Columbia

"Dr. Samantha Nutt is a force of nature. A courageous and tireless advocate for human rights. Her colorful, revealing and heart-wrenching first-hand accounts are a must read for anyone who's given so much as a penny to an NGO."

> – RAINE MAIDA, lead singer, Our Lady Peace, songwriter, and activist

"Extremely perceptive and original. . . . Nutt deftly skewers pretensions, complacencies and, often disturbingly, imperial assumptions of the aid world." *– Globe and Mail*

DAMNED NATIONS

GREED, GUNS, ARMIES, & AID

SAMANTHA NUTT, M.D.

SIGNAL
MCCLELLAND
& STEWART

Copyright © 2011 by Samantha Nutt

Cloth edition published 2011
Paperback edition first published 2012
This Signal paperback edition published 2018

Signal is an imprint of McClelland & Stewart,
a division of Random House of Canada Limited

Library and Archives Canada Cataloguing in Publication data available upon request.

ISBN 978-0-7710-5144-9
EBOOK ISBN 978-0-7710-5147-0

Published simultaneously in the United States of America by
McClelland & Stewart, a division of Random House of Canada Limited

Library of Congress Control Number: 2012932381

Cover design: Rachel Cooper
Cover image © MUNIR UZ ZAMAN/AFP/Getty images

Typeset in Van Dijck by M&S, Toronto
Printed and bound in the United States of America

McClelland & Stewart,
a division of Random House of Canada Limited,
a Penguin Random House Company
www.penguinrandomhouse.ca

1 2 3 4 5   22 21 20 19 18

FOR ERIC HOSKINS,

my partner in this journey,

AND OUR BEAUTIFUL SON, RHYS.

In memory of

Margaret Hassan and Aquila al-Hashimi.

Peace is not only better than war, but infinitely more arduous.

George Bernard Shaw

CONTENTS

AUTHOR'S NOTE

The stories contained within this book span nearly two decades of my work with war-torn communities around the world. During this time, I have been privileged to meet extraordinary individuals whose courage and compassion transcend any attempt on my part to introduce them to you in these pages. But I have tried to honour their legacy by providing a narrative platform through which they might speak directly to you and hopefully inspire you, as they did me. In some cases, I was able to rely on detailed notes (so long as I was able to read my own hand-written scrawl). In other instances, I relied on memory. Some of these memories are chillingly pronounced for me, as I have been replaying them in my head for years. Where the details have faded, I have written the dialogue as I remember it to give you a sense of the overall content and tone of the conversation – and the impression it made.

Public figures and personalities are named. However, I have changed the names and some of the identifying details of all who confided in me or revealed truths about their lives that could endanger them, or otherwise cause harm. In this new edition of *Damned Nations*, I also have updated – where possible – facts and figures referenced in the original publication.

The views expressed in this book are entirely my own and do not reflect those of *any* humanitarian organization or academic institution that has kindly employed me over the years (and that, with any luck, does not now regret that decision).

PREFACE

'Cause hope, boys, is a cheap thing, cheap thing.
DAVID BOWIE, "SWEET THING"

I wrote this book *before*. Before the war in Syria. Before ISIS. Before Libya unspooled as a much-touted example of NATO resolve to crush tyranny and emerged as a seaside haven for human traffickers and Al-Qaeda operatives. Before Boko Haram became a household name for its kidnapping of African school-children. Before the largest famine and refugee crisis since World War II. Before terror attacks on ordinary citizens enjoying a marathon, concert, patio, or promenade in the world's most famous cities felt grievously commonplace. Before *President* became a prefix to the name Donald Trump.

How did we get here? In rereading the pages of this book it is not difficult to spot the large, blinding, megawatt arrows pointing to the place in which the world now finds itself. If there is one costly and incontrovertible lesson from the 2003 Iraq War — and which might have foreshadowed the violence that later beset Libya and Syria — it is that open, democratic societies do not readily emerge from the ruins of Western-backed exercises in regime change. It is a lamentable reality that sometimes the only thing keeping deeply divided states from collapse — artificially cobbled together by imperial powers in the first instance — is authoritarian rule. These are places where civilians are tortured and murdered by the state with relative impunity. They are also tortured and murdered *after* their oppressors have been tossed from their gilded palaces and protected enclaves – by vengeful neighbours, dissident militias, terrorist groups, and a new power elite intent on asserting their own religious or ethnic dominance. And, whether as cause or effect, such lawless, angry abysses are a natural habitat for extremists, who hide within the chaos to recruit and mobilize with irrepressible zeal.

There are ways to avert such catastrophes, but this is long, arduous work that is consistently overlooked in favour of more muscular responses: annual worldwide military spending is now at its highest point since the Cold War, averaging $1.7 trillion a year. By comparison, this spending is twelve times higher than total global contributions to humanitarian aid for impoverished nations – money spent on averting the starvation of millions of people, economic development, women's rights, clean water, refugees, vaccination programs, and on ensuring children can go to school. Hard power approaches, from advanced weapons systems to sophisticated intelligence gathering, have won the day. To argue otherwise is as fruitless as arguing against technology: it marches on with or without your participation. Nevertheless, states that launch foreign wars, whether under the pretext of neutralizing international threats or protecting civilians from abuse and atrocity (even in cases where the evidence for "just cause" is irrefutable) should know by now that without peace, everyone loses. That takes effort, energy, and money – a lot of it. So why is one side of this equation constantly receiving the lion's share of available resources – after all, there is only one bucket to drink from – if the objective is to reduce the overall risk of violence and terrorism? Saying "War costs more." is a lazy answer because there are only so many wars to fight, whereas the possibilities for investing in reconstruction, reconciliation, democratic development, health care, and social welfare for at-risk populations are nearly infinite. Therefore only two possible explanations exist, which are not mutually exclusive: either chronic conflict is the end goal, reinforcing global power structures and buttressing economies that own a major stake in Eisenhower's broadly defined military-industrial complex; or too many of our world leaders are not learning from past mistakes.

The value of the legal arms trade alone during the fifteen years following 9/11 has steadily increased to almost double its former levels – to $31 billion a year by 2016 – though the real number is likely much higher given Russia's and China's laxity in reporting. Eighty percent of those weapons came from the five permanent members of the United Nations Security Council (P5), plus Germany. It can be argued these sales were a necessary response to the war on terror, but given that most arms have a long shelf life, why would the production of so many more of them be required every year? While the number of countries locked in civil war during that period didn't significantly change, terror, certainly, was an ongoing threat. But if the militarized strategy was working to any appreciable degree, then the global demand for arms logically should have shown – after a decade and a half – signs of abating. This growth in sales can't be explained away by a stronger U.S. dollar or increased production costs either: the absolute number of weapons systems, including vehicles, ships, and aircraft sold during this period increased as well. And to suggest that this was because there were more terrorists to fight as well as ongoing wars in Iraq and Afghanistan merely proves the point: increased weapons and military spending have not reduced the threat of war or terrorism throughout the world. A more plausible explanation is that sales maintained their upward trajectory in part because of where some of these weapons ended up; arms and ammunition recovered from ISIS- and Taliban-held territories are now known to have been manufactured in Russia, China, Eastern Europe, and the United States. The West's three-year effort to crush ISIS notwithstanding, Russia has spent untold billions propping up its puppet, Syria's Bashar al-Assad, while protecting him militarily from some of these very same medieval misogynists (and for the time being, from prosecution for war crimes). China is not so much agnostic about who it sells arms to as it is utterly incapable of embarrassment – a perk of state-controlled media and never having to face a cynical electorate. It is a perfect circle of supply and demand that would have made John Maynard Keynes blush: governments underwrite wars that rely on weapons we manufactured to defeat those with weapons we manufactured. No wonder so many North American public pension plans continue to have holdings in the world's biggest domestic and international arms manufacturers – it is a recession-proof investment*.

How quickly peace, even as a word, has come to feel nostalgic, almost quaint. Freedom has to be "defended." Terror must be "defeated." There are red lines, drone strikes, and the occasional my-missile-is-bigger-than-yours Twitter exchanges between heads of state. Diplomacy, disarmament, and multilateralism cannot compete with crass dick jokes, even when the taunts involve *real*

---

* In 2017, the Canadian Pension Plan Investment Board had in excess of $1 billion in holdings in thirty-seven of the world's top one hundred arms manufacturers. Thirty state-managed pension funds in the United States have more than $2.5 billion in combined investments in three of the biggest weapons and ammunitions manufacturers, including Lockheed Martin, Northrop Grumman Corporation, and Raytheon.

nuclear warheads. It doesn't matter that millions of lives hang in the balance — there is no room for equivocation in this show of strength and force. This isn't just a Trumpian phenomenon. Some of the most progressive politicians of the past decade also have been the most hawkish. It was Hillary Clinton, as secretary of state, whose eventual call for military intervention in Libya sealed the deal for NATO. It was the Obama administration that ended up accidentally arming the Al-Qaeda–linked Al-Nursa Front in Syria after their attempts to prop up moderate opposition fighters failed. And it was Canada's feminist Prime Minister, Justin Trudeau, whose government signed off on a fifteen billion dollar–arms deal with Saudi Arabia, even as that regime lay waste to Houthi villages in Yemen and blocked humanitarian access to two million Yemeni children at grave risk of dying from malnutrition and starvation. Left or Right, the prevailing orthodoxy remains the same: Western militaries save the world from terror, and they fight for our social and political freedoms at home and abroad.

Who would openly disagree with such an assertion, except maybe a handful of fringy socialists, a few hard-core libertarians who deplore all taxation (wars are expensive), and some earnest grandmothers in French berets heavy with "Carter Mondale" pins? Who doesn't want to feel *safer*?

In reality things are much more complicated. Far from making us safer, the ongoing prioritization of military responses over the pursuit of other strategies (be they diplomatic or humanitarian) is a missed opportunity of critical consequence. I am neither a terrorist sympathizer nor any kind of apologist for despots and dictators — that such declarations are necessary shows how far the pendulum has swung. However, the one thing I have learned consistently and irrefutably, from the almost quarter century I have now spent working in and out of war zones, is that preventing terrorism and atrocity in the first instance is much easier than attempting to contain it after the fact. And until this becomes the urgent priority, the cycle will never end.

When I reflect on the slow-motion tragedy that followed the U.S. military's invasion of Iraq (and which is explored at length in these pages), it is easy to understand how ISIS was able to establish a caliphate that, at its peak, occupied one hundred thousand square kilometres spanning two nations. Deposing Saddam Hussein, far from unleashing democracy across the Arab world as members of the Bush administration once incredulously believed, only intensified violence and oppression throughout the region. American-backed efforts to remake the Iraqi government, while deliberately excluding groups previously aligned with the former dictator, made Iran – not the U.S. or its allies – the prime beneficiary of the Iraq War. Not surprisingly, Saudi Arabia and other Gulf States, fearing an expanded Iranian influence on their doorsteps, responded by engaging in proxy wars that already have ensnared Syria, Yemen, Lebanon, and Turkey. The displacement of Syrian and Iraqi refugees has also had a destabilizing impact on Jordan – arguably the U.S.'s most strategically significant Arab ally in the region. Israel too has felt the pressures of living beside an emboldened, Iranian-friendly Hezbollah. The fallout even has extended to European nations that have been dealing with a migration crises along their own borders, the scale of which has not been seen in more than seventy years. The Kurds, persecuted and gassed by Saddam Hussein and a critical U.S. partner in both the 2003 Iraq War and the 2017 offensive against ISIS, are under siege from all sides. Instead of reducing the threat of terror, the 2003 U.S.-led war dangerously amplified it, because the regional and historical contexts were either poorly understood, or worse, simply ignored. Military actions since then largely have been coordinated efforts in damage control.

Meanwhile, on the ground in Iraq, local resentments festered in a climate of heightened insecurity. Over the past decade, these resentments were most pronounced among young men – especially those belonging to Iraq's minority Sunnis, who felt stigmatized and excluded by the central government in Bagdad. Among Iraq's Sunnis' litany of grievances was their mistreatment and torture in U.S. military prisons (and which produced more than two dozen of ISIS' senior leaders*), and the ostentatious profiteering in the oil and reconstruction sectors – mostly at the hands of American military and energy contractors. KBR, formerly Kellogg Brown & Root, DynCorp International, and Fluor Corporation – three large American military contractors – alone earned more than $50 billion from the Iraq War. (KBR is a former Halliburton subsidiary, which paid one of the war's architects – Dick Cheney – "back pay" and bonuses of close to $2 million while he was the sitting vice president.) These dissident groups also had a common enemy: the Iranian-aligned Shia "apostates" ensconced in Iraq's parliament and the Western "infidels" who'd handed them the keys. The veracity of these claims mattered less than their impact: religious zealots, a splinter group of genocidal extremists for whom Al-Qaeda had grown too soft, and

---

* I recognize the corollary also holds true: that these men were in U.S. military prisons precisely because they were considered a threat, and therefore it wasn't the incarceration that was the central problem, but rather their release that provided the enabling environment. However, the radicalizing effect of prisons is now well established, with ISIS fighters confirming senior ISIS officials such as Abu Ahmed al-Kuwaiti and Abu Bakr al-Baghdadi actively recruited members while incarcerated under U.S. command in Iraq.

some of Saddam Hussein's most ruthless former officials leveraged them to their fullest advantage. This is how ISIS was born. It was not a mystery. The warning signs were everywhere.

ISIS also came of age during the dawn of social media, the benefits of which were quickly understood. Social media and dark web platforms allowed the group's leadership and acolytes to digitally weaponize their grievances to ensnare other mostly young men who felt just as stigmatized and isolated by the very same Western governments and their liberal societies. That so many of these countries also had welcomed some of their parents as immigrants and refugees was beside the point: here was an emerging online community that made them feel superior, wanted, and accepted, all the while stoking their rage and grooming them to deploy it. Identical tactics have been used by every hateful, misogynistic, and ultranationalist group – from the Patriotic Front to the English Defence League and National Action – to have sprouted up in recent years across Europe and North America. They all traffic in self-righteousness and a disturbing vision of racial and ideological homogeneity that promises their followers a spot at the top of the heap of human existence. And each leverages the other's rhetoric and violence ("Muslims are attacking our country."; "Infidels are killing our babies with their Zionist bombs.") to justify their irredentism. Terrorist movements like ISIS and the West's angry reactionaries benefit from each other's existence. Their depraved codependence is one of the saddest and most terrifying paradoxes of our time.

The ongoing lesson here is war and terrorism have many precursors, few of which will be solved by the trifecta of guns, drones, and Navy SEALs. There is no sophisticated weaponry that instantly can restore health care, education, law and order, and good governance – the essential ingredients for social stability. And no NATO-led interventions or threats will end centuries-old ethnic, religious, and territorial disputes – particularly when P5 member states are willing to arm so many of the parties to such conflicts. Peace requires consistent, painstaking, and strategic effort coupled with a deep knowledge of history as well as human nature, which perhaps best explains why the world's power brokers so easily default to dominance and control. And media coverage, in an era of consolidation and online click bait, does little to dispel such notions. "One thousand young Afghan men in Taliban-held areas find employment in alternatives to the opium trade after two years of intensive education and skills training tied to market demands" is not nearly as delectable a headline as "Hundreds of Taliban fighters targeted in drone attacks as poppy fields razed." And yet, only one of these approaches holds any promise of disrupting the cycle of violence, impunity, and extremism besetting that war-ravaged nation. Repeated efforts to kill these young men only feeds the supply chain, amplifying the cries for revenge felt across borders and generations.

A year ago, I returned to Iraq after a prolonged absence. This was the war I could no longer face. The violent deaths of my two mentors and friends in Iraq fourteen years prior, Aquila al-Hashimi and Margaret Hassan – bold, courageous, and brilliant women whose stories are featured in these pages – had left me profoundly doubting everything I had once believed about the primacy of humanitarian intervention in times of war. I started to wonder whether I had been peddling a lie: that humanitarian aid could do anything to stop, or even mitigate, the devastation and abject suffering. After all, the very concept of a neutral humanitarian space had been permanently and irrevocably shattered in the aftermath of the 2003 Iraq War. Aid workers and journalists were being raped, kidnapped, and killed with alarming frequency. We had become pawns, unwittingly transforming into a renewable resource for militant groups in Iraq, Yemen, Afghanistan, the Philippines, Syria, Sudan, the Sahel region and elsewhere, who were reaping millions in ransom payouts – funds that were then used to buy arms, and with appalling irony, wage more war. And while some aid workers were being taken hostage, others – like Doctors Without Borders staff in Afghanistan – were being targeted in full and flagrant violation of international law. A century of human rights infrastructure was coming undone, along with my previously held convictions. Did I *really* think unarmed humanitarians could do their jobs effectively and free from threat or coercion in unstable parts of the world? Did I *really* still believe aid organizations – be they local or international – were changing anything, or were even capable of changing anything in places of perpetual war? Was I *really* willing, with a young son at home, to continue taking the necessary risks in order to find out?

Returning to Iraq just seemed to amplify this sense of futility. The first thing I said on arrival, rather bluntly and unsentimentally, when I was met by War Child staff member Nikki Whaites – a veteran of the world's war zones herself – was "Everyone I knew here is dead." Her response was exactly what someone with our shared history would say: "Well, we aren't going to solve that today, now are we? So let's just get in the car and get on with it." She was right, of course: when confronted by grief, fear, and doubt, all you can do is get on with it, because – as I also learned from my father's sudden passing – such loss can never be fixed. The only option is to move forward and hope the hurt eventually dissipates.

Erbil, the capital of Iraqi Kurdistan, is an hour's drive from Mosul (ISIS' epicentre in Iraq, where they had formed government and even collected taxes), where Kurdish and Iraqi troops, buttressed by American, Canadian, and other international forces, were bringing ISIS to its heels. The stories recounted by young girls and women who had escaped ISIS, but especially those from Yazidi and other minority communities in Iraq, revealed a level of depravity and sociopathy among the terror group's soldiers and commanders that was as widespread as it was horrifying. When I met with some of these young women and their families, most had mothers, sisters, or daughters who were still missing. Girls barely into adolescence had been ripped from their families, raped repeatedly, gifted to ISIS recruits, and roped together and sold in markets. They were treated as spoils of war and thus – in the puritanical interpretation of Sunni Islam that ISIS' adherents followed – could be kept as slaves, assaulted, traded, or disposed of at whim. ("Sanctioned by God" are three of the most dangerous words in any language.) For many, the nightmare continued even once they were freed, as they were widely perceived within their traditional, rural families to be damaged goods. ISIS were not the only militants to exploit such tactics, which have also been widely used in the eastern Democratic Republic of Congo and South Sudan – two other countries embroiled in protracted, ethnically-charged wars. However, ISIS systematized sexual violence with such ruthless efficiency that generational renewal would become impossible for many of Iraq's minority communities.

As the military push to liberate Mosul progressed, Sunni families who had stayed behind after ISIS seized control began to flee*. The problem was how to sort the hardline elements from the mass of civilians who themselves were victims of ISIS' campaign of terror and intimidation. Sunni women and girls were easy enough to clear, but men and boys of fighting age were another matter altogether. It's important to note while some of these young men were most certainly active and willing ISIS participants, others were not. In a war zone, however, you often don't get to decide. If a well-organized, violent, angry group of armed militants rolled into town and started executing those whose allegiance and affiliations were in question, most civilians would respond by doing just about anything to be spared – if not for themselves, then for their loved ones. If that means growing a beard and handing over money and the car keys, so be it. And if it means letting your ten-year-old run the occasional errand when an ISIS commander barks at him from the street to fetch some water, because if he doesn't, he might just shoot the child on the spot as he has countless others, most of us would

---

* Prior to ISIS, Mosul was Iraq's third-largest city. Many stayed behind for a variety of reasons, many more practical than ideological: elderly parents too infirm to flee; houses and other lifetime investments that otherwise would have been appropriated; a not unreasonable belief that they would face violence and persecution themselves as minority Sunnis at the hands of groups seeking revenge for ISIS' actions; fears of outside arrest and detention for having friends, neighbours, or distant relatives who had joined ISIS, and so on. One elderly woman living in an internally displaced person camp in a suburban neighbourhood of Mosul told me she stayed knowing ISIS was on its way into town for the most banal reason of all: her husband couldn't get the car to start and their kids lived too far away. They thought they would drive out in a day or two, but by that point ISIS soldiers were busy making examples of those trying to flee by shooting them in the head and suspending their bodies from trees and monuments. And so, as many Iraqis have done for decades at the hands of autocratic rulers, this couple decided to go along to get along.

acquiesce to that too – if nervously and reluctantly. The survival instinct in times of war is riddled with excruciating compromises. For many families living under ISIS' control, that is exactly what happened: they stayed alive by not resisting ISIS' attempts to indoctrinate their children in their religious schools; when beckoned, they tended to ISIS fighters and cooked their meals; and they even, some of them, attended weapons training led by ISIS commanders because every able-bodied male who didn't participate automatically aroused suspicion. There is no question some of those in Mosul were there because they enthusiastically embraced ISIS' agenda, hated what their country had become, held bigoted views of Iraq's minorities, and wanted to reassert their social and political dominance. The point here is local support for ISIS existed in degrees, and those degrees were hard to differentiate among the stampede of people fleeing during the months-long military advance to quash the former caliphate. No one could be trusted: young men least of all.

As Iraqi, Iranian, and Kurdish forces – with backing from the American, Canadian, European, and Australian militaries – wrestled with the burdensome task of sifting the salt from the sand, those not deemed a threat (largely women and young children) were housed in internally displaced person (IDP) camps under Kurdish authority. These camps were heavily monitored and controlled, not unreasonably under the circumstances, by local special security forces. What to do with the men and adolescent boys was much more complicated. Some had surrendered but were known fighters even if they were legally child soldiers at the time. These young men and boys were separated from their families and sent to undisclosed locations, or black sites, also under the authority of local special security forces. It is not known how many of these young men and boys entered these mysterious interrogation centres and were never heard from again. Eventually, the *Toronto Star* and ABC News obtained and published photographs of detainees being tortured at these black sites – photos that were eerily reminiscent of those taken fifteen years earlier at Abu Ghraib. Detainees who did make it out were then transferred to established prison facilities to await trial.

———

THE BOYS FROM MOSUL housed in one of Iraq's few juvenile detention centres are a feral bunch who, nevertheless, have settled into a social hierarchy: there are the silent, muscular brooders bookending the talkative charmers in the centre; the twitchy, scrawny hangers-on fidgeting at the margins; and the quiet dreamers in the back row, their minds wandering in and out of the conversation like birds returning to a nest. The boys speak for themselves and for each other. They were brought to the prison after a month, give or take (days are hard to track under such circumstances), of what they describe as torture at the hands of local special security forces. None is older than sixteen, and only a couple of them have been allowed to have telephone contact with their families since their captivity. They tell a remarkably consistent story, despite being accused of dramatically different levels of co-operation with ISIS: their hands were roped together behind their backs; these ropes were then pulled upwards like a slingshot ready to fire, as the full weight of their bodies hung beneath them*. Who did they know? Who were

---

* It is worth noting that I met with these boys several months *before* the story broke in May, 2017, of adults alleging identical means and methods of torture in these very same black sites. There would have been little or no opportunity for these boys to have learned about these incidents except from firsthand experience.

the ISIS commanders and collaborators? Where were they from? What did the boys see? Who did the commanders meet with? All the while, barking demands for names, names, names. One boy acknowledged he named his own brother just so it would stop, even though he claimed they were both innocent. Another said his brother had done the same to him, and that was why he had been arrested. Cousins, school friends, neighbours – a name, even without merit, was a cry of "mercy." Two boys told a different story. Tearfully, they struggled to talk about the electrical probes that were attached to their genitals. The cramping shocks. The humiliation and degradation they felt. The youngest of these boys was thirteen. He had not been allowed to speak to his parents and wondered whether they knew he was alive. The only lawyers the boys had access to were those chosen by local special security forces, as they were to stand trial in a special security forces court, with a special security forces–appointed judge. Hearing this caused me to count the number of times the boys used *special security forces* in one sentence, but the gist was this: Iraqis were building their own Guantanamo, complete with a kangaroo court. The boys' legal situation was further complicated by Iraq's Byzantine rules surrounding children and the death penalty. While minors cannot be executed, under Iraqi law they still can be sentenced to death and be executed at any point after their eighteenth birthday. Terrorism charges in Iraq, but in particular charges of supporting ISIS, are considered a capital offense.

Human Rights Watch later would report on the allegations these boys made about their detention and subsequent torture, minus some of the more graphic details. I have been doing this work for far too long to believe the majority of young boys and men who claim they were only carrying water or changing bandages while their compatriots lay waste to entire villages. But I do believe them when they say they were tortured, physically and sexually, at the hands of militaries that American, Canadian, and European forces aligned themselves with in order to defeat ISIS. And while these may be some of the compromises citizens of liberal democracies are prepared to make to avoid being blown up on the subway or run over in public squares, it does beg the question: How does this end? These young boys were being kept thirty to a cell designed for six. Among them were boys who had seen and done much more than they were admitting to, and who had been inundated with ISIS' ideological propaganda every day for three years. None now had access to school, or family, or any of the other things necessary to nurture healthy, well-adjusted adults. Under international law, it is unlawful for armed groups to recruit and deploy children, and they are entitled to rehabilitation, reunification (with their families), and reintegration (back into society). These kinds of recovery programs have been widely used in Sierra Leone, Liberia, South Sudan and while they often are imperfectly administered (in part due to a lack of continuity in funding and support), they still offer child combatants the best chance of recovery while reducing the broader threat they present to their communities. Even if these boys from Mosul are ever released – which in the current climate is a long shot – what kind of lives will they lead with no education and no prospects? The more radicalized agents among them have nothing but time on their hands and prison yards overflowing with young, impressionable minds who have every reason to hate those who put them there. The boys' families, too, have good reason to be bitter and resentful.

I have long argued that it is war's proponents, and not its detractors, who are naive to its complexities and ramifications.

That's not to suggest that military intervention was not necessary in order to deny ISIS the territorial and economic base that sustained them. However, there can never be security without peace, and there can never be peace without a dramatic shift in global approaches to violence and instability. The fundamental grievances that ISIS so successfully tapped into remain in Iraq and Syria, and among some groups, have hardened. There already is a regional war under way in the Middle East and the threat of ongoing civil war remains high. ISIS supporters and fighters are finding fertile ground in Libya, Yemen, and Afghanistan. Boko Haram, a terror group in Nigeria that has kidnapped five thousand children over the past fifteen years, has also pledged allegiance. The war against ISIS in Iraq and Syria certainly disrupted the problem, but it has not solved it.

Not every war or terror movement will be prevented by increased development and aid spending, employment, robust diplomacy, rigorous arms control and disarmament measures, access to justice, and local reconciliation efforts. Terrorism in particular is a global phenomenon that has myriad complex drivers and risk factors (especially cases involving "lone wolf" actors who often are dually afflicted by mental health concerns). But in countries formerly locked in conflict where some of these approaches have been put into practice – Sierra Leone, Colombia, Liberia, Mozambique, and northern Uganda, for example – there has not yet been a return to civil war. I add *yet* here because every country on that list could benefit from additional aid spending, governmental reform, and economic development for these gains to hold. There is no denying, as well, that there are serious problems with the way aid monies are spent and how humanitarian programs are administered. Aid, and more broadly humanitarian intervention, are grounded in outdated practices and geopolitical privilege that, too often, become the blunt instrument of neocolonialism. I review these concerns further in Chapters Four and Five, however, more recent events have caused some dramatic shifts in what is often called the "aid movement" that also are worth mentioning.

In early 2018, one of the world's oldest and most reputable humanitarian organizations, Oxfam, came under intense scrutiny for its handling of expatriate staff in Haiti after the 2011 earthquake who were alleged to have exploited local women for sex. The men were sent packing, but at the time Oxfam did not publicly acknowledge what had transpired, and the men involved went on to other postings with different humanitarian agencies working on the front lines with vulnerable women and children. As the story gathered momentum, it turned out many of the world's most established and reputable relief and development organizations, including UN agencies, had dealt with sexual predators in their midst. This surprised almost no one within the aid community, and based on the ensuing media frenzy, almost everyone outside of it. The emergency aid sector has always been a magnet for rootless, risk-taking men with a god complex. And the more dangerous and remote the posting, the fewer means there are to regularly monitor that behaviour, and generally speaking, the more desperate and impoverished the locals are.

This disparity in access to power and resources between foreign personnel running aid programs and those they serve is enormous and governs every interaction between these two groups, right down to the level of who receives food, medicine, shelter, and asylum. Even for me, as a woman working in these environments, I have felt like fresh meat walking into the hyena den. Although age does have its advantages in this respect, as these days I am probably closer to roadkill than prime rib, which means I am happily left to my own devices a lot more often. Still, it isn't hard to imagine how a teenage girl in Haiti who's lost everything must feel. But as non-governmental organizations wrestle with how best to protect vulnerable groups under this care, one thing has become abundantly clear: the old way of foreigners rushing in to deliver aid – faces gruff, brows sweaty, stethoscopes draped over muscular shoulders – is over. The emphasis has to be on building up the capacity and opportunities that exist within country, starting with women. And their increased social and political capital is exactly the counterbalance needed not only to reduce the ongoing risk of sexual exploitation and harassment in high-risk environments, but also to ultimately transition countries from conflict. That is the future of aid, and frankly it cannot get here fast enough.

Over the past five years the world has pivoted towards greater violence and instability. Technology, social media especially, has been a Faustian bargain: knowledge and information have never been more accessible, but so are hate and terror groups. It seems to me – if the political landscape in America is a bellwether of broader social trends – we are shouting more and understanding less. This will only further stoke anger and violence. Whether it is a permanent shift or a temporary detour in the long march of human progress remains to be seen. One thing, though, is certain: we cannot shoot, bomb, or bully our way out of it.

INTRODUCTION

The parts of me that used to think I was different
or smarter or whatever, almost made me die.
DAVID FOSTER WALLACE

When war returned to Bukavu, in the eastern Democratic Republic of Congo along the Rwandan border, I dismissed the gunfire as nothing more than a minor skirmish. A peace accord had been signed eighteen months earlier by most of the fractured parties to this hellish conflict. *Had no one read it?* Maybe, I reasoned, it was just a group of boys not quite satisfied with the terms of their severance from one of the ever-shifting rebel groups. *This isn't serious. It will pass.* During my previous mission to the region a few months earlier, there had been hushed chatter among aid workers of a "third revolution," but war zones are full of such stories – of final chapters in battle not yet written. And, by all accounts, the rumours predated the peace process, so there was no need for concern. There were 10,000 United Nations peacekeepers in the region, and I was confident it wouldn't take them long to identify the problem and contain it.

I was travelling with a documentary crew, gathering footage for an hour-long feature on the Congo's devastating war. Our team was set to leave the next day, so I returned to my room at the Orchid Hotel – a Belgian-run *auberge* on the sluggish shores of Lake Kivu – and continued packing. Half of our crew, which included my husband, Eric Hoskins, had not yet returned from filming. I did not expect to hear these words at my door: "Sam, Eric's been detained. Security officials are holding him and the rest of the team at the police station, and have confiscated their passports and equipment. They want to see our footage." Eric was negotiating for the others to be released after they were stopped for filming in the streets, and was offering himself up as collateral until the officials obtained what they wanted. We had UN permission to film, and this kind of brazen harassment of independent witnesses with camera gear is too often the prelude to atrocity. It was only then that I realized the gunfire we were hearing was a call to arms.

I made a list of discrete tasks: grab a few tapes of footage unlikely to be deemed sensitive and whatever cash we had left; call our contacts at the UN; and, quickly, find someone at the hotel who could take me to the police station. The roads in front of the Orchid were rapidly degrading into battle lines. It was no longer just the crackle of automatic fire I heard; there was the pitched whistling of bullets as well. *They're getting closer.* It was a resurgence of violence that no one was expecting or could explain. Even hotel guests from the American embassy in Kinshasa, who presumably had access to sophisticated intelligence reports, were caught off guard and could provide little information.

I was on the third task, about to climb into the back of a wheezing old Peugeot, when Eric came running towards me from another vehicle. "Get behind a wall!" he shouted. "There are soldiers everywhere. They've started shooting." Eric had lived through a violent coup in Sudan, and his instincts were unquestionably better than mine. As relieved as I was to see him, it was not the time to tell him.

2

We ran between two buildings. I was unfocused, rushing through different scenarios in my mind, none of them useful and all of them compounding my mounting anxiety. I'd faced several close calls in war zones before this one – attempted car ambushes, the sudden appearance of menacing men in berets and mirrored sunglasses – but never one in which I'd had time to *think*. And it's only when you have time to think, unarmed in the midst of a fierce gunfight, that you understand how utterly and hopelessly fucked you really are.

During a lull in the shooting, Eric and I scrambled to the hotel lobby to find the other members of our team, none of whom had any war experience. It was then that I learned he and the others had escaped after convincing the security officials to follow them to the hotel to view the footage. Once confronted by the violence in the streets, their captors fled in the other direction. The team's vehicle pressed on, fearing it would be more dangerous to remain separated from the rest of us.

After a torturous night of uninterrupted gunfire and sporadic shelling, a few more details emerged. The Congolese military had arrested a couple of Rwandan soldiers at the border crossing a short distance from our hotel, reigniting the conflict (it wasn't clear which armed group they were associated with). Residents in the area were now trapped between these warring factions as they took shots at one another, and the only thing we could do was take cover and wait.

By late morning, the shelling had begun to intensify. Bullets ricocheted through the hotel kitchen window. Along with everyone else, Eric and I made frantic calls to UN authorities, trying to assess the security of our location and wondering whether we should risk moving. Unbelievably, the Internet in the business office was still working, and I managed to send a couple of emails to my mother in Toronto: "Everything okay. Departure slightly delayed. Back in a couple of days." We have an unstated arrangement when I'm in the field: I don't tell her where I'm going and she doesn't ask, so long as I send her regular emails letting her know I'm alive. The advice we received from United Nations and Canadian government contacts over the phone was consistent: "Stay where you are, keep your heads down, and stand by for further instructions." Two guests from the hotel came running up from the garden area saying they'd come under fire by the water's edge. No one was injured, but it was an ominous warning: it meant we were in the militias' crosshairs.

Shortly afterwards, it sounded as if the rocket-propelled grenades (RPGs) were landing dangerously close – so close that I immediately dropped to the floor, prompting an unflinching Congolese man in the lobby, who'd obviously endured much worse, to jokingly say, "I see you do not enjoy the beautiful music we play here in the Congo." It is still one of the most reassuring things anyone has ever said to me in the midst of a crisis.

A few of the hotel staff had access to a small but impressively reinforced "panic room," while the rest of us huddled together in what we deemed to be the safest area: a cramped guest room on the lowest level of the hotel, built into the side of a hilly ridge and protected on three sides. Of course, if an errant RPG were to have landed in the hotel lobby above our heads, the entire building would have collapsed upon us. Despite reassurances from UN officials that we were "not the targets" and therefore not likely to take a direct hit, a significant proportion of the roving armed groups were drunk and stoned teenage boys whose weapons training would have been limited to "Pull here." Whether we were targets or not, the boys' spectacularly bad aim was worth heeding.

4

At first, we casually mingled in the room, introducing ourselves to the other thirty or so people who'd taken refuge along with our team – local hotel staff, guests, and others who happened to be visiting when the shooting started and the roads became impassable. UN helicopters beat overhead and for hours it sounded as if the front line had landed right on top of us. During a momentary reprieve we filed out of the room, only to be forced back in by a sudden and dramatic escalation of explosions.

Eric and I crouched with the other members of our team at the back of the room, pressed against an armoire. People huddled together in the bathroom and under furniture, staying low to the floor. Mortars were landing on the hotel grounds. With each forceful bang, fine fragments of plaster showered down on us. But the worst was about to happen: the sound of running above our heads. Urgent, confused steps were heard between the eruptions of gunfire. Doors were repeatedly opened, then slammed – whoever it was, however many there were, they appeared to be searching for something, or someone. No one dared speak. A man by the window reached above his head and gently pulled the curtain closed. Eric and I looked at one another, and I could tell by the pained expression on his face that we were having the same thought: "They're in the building." There was one other woman in the room – an American embassy employee. I knew it wouldn't be long before she and I would be dragged outside and raped. And what would happen to the men? Some would be mercilessly killed as a statement about who's really in charge of the eastern Democratic Republic of Congo. Others would be shot so that an itinerant group of pubescent boys might feel the rush of holding absolute power over life and death. After what had been a decade together, I knew that under no circumstances would Eric submit to the violence and degradation making its way towards us. More than anything, I wanted to tell him that he needn't be brave, that brave meant certain death, and survival was all that mattered. Then, another bone-shattering bang, after which the footsteps could be heard directly outside our window. I couldn't breathe.

Fear, in war, is absolute.

More than two hundred people were killed during the outbreak of armed conflict in Bukavu that cornered our team in late May 2004. To my shock and surprise (and enduring gratitude), it was not a group of rebel soldiers behind the door but a Canadian volunteer peacekeeper, Chuck Pelletier, armed only with a short wooden baton, the price tag still conspicuously attached. He'd been staying at the hotel on temporary assignment and was in regular communication with MONUC (the United Nations Organization Mission in the Democratic Republic of Congo) operatives. When it became clear that the risk had escalated, the UN peacekeeping force deployed armoured personnel carriers (APCs) through the crossfire to collect everyone trapped at the Orchid. They had already moved many residents from our street, as combatants had attacked homes a few doors away from the hotel, raping and shooting civilians. Chuck organized us into numbered teams, then, in groups of seven, we ran single file to the APCs as the volleys continued. At MONUC headquarters, we joined hundreds of others fleeing the violence. The UN made no distinction or special accommodations for internationals, who were mostly Belgians, Americans, and Canadians, which is as it should always be in such circumstances. Congolese and foreigners trapped in insecure areas, including the Orchid, were evacuated together and treated with equal consideration at all times.

As the sun began to set, UN personnel announced there

would be a distribution of mats to women only. The covered areas were overflowing with evacuees, and the only available space was outside on the lawn beside an exhausted contingent of South African peacekeepers. Under normal circumstances, I would have protested the decision to give mats just to women. And as the only woman on our team, I didn't want the guilt of reclining comfortably on my spoils in front of my stiff-upper-lipped compatriots. But once I realized the temperature was dropping, I was wearing a useless T-shirt, and the grass we'd be sleeping on was wet, I got over myself. "We'll share it!" I announced to the others as I sheepishly trundled off, elbows up. (True to my word, we took turns throughout the night.)

The next day the UN began to move people to the other side of town in buses under armed escort. Areas of Bukavu through to the airport were reasonably secure, and MONUC wanted to avoid turning their compound into a displaced people's camp. During a briefing by a MONUC representative after boarding the bus, in which we were told to rest our heads on our knees and our hands over our faces in the event of bullets flying through windows, he declared that we were "not to panic," but he would be making the journey with us "lying face down on the floor." This, he explained, was so that, in the "unlikely event that our driver is shot, I may resume driving." Our bus driver didn't say a word, but he flashed his boss a look that read, "Here's a better idea, asshole: I'll lie on the floor and *you* go first."

To say I am lucky to be alive doesn't fully capture the extent to which I recognize this to be true, for as long as I can claim it to be. And hopefully, I'm not nearly done yet. Most of us come into this world amidst a frenzy of pain and emotion and unpredictability, and too many of us leave in the same way. If between the two certitudes of birth and death lies a generous period of love,

7

family, and friendships, free from the shackles of violence and poverty, it is a life to be coveted. War, and the pursuit of war, destroys us. It turns teenagers into killers, neighbours into *génocidaires*, and politicians into executioners. War is humanity at its most primitive, despite our attempts to dress it up, distance ourselves from it through technology, and frame it in acceptable terms – a battle for good in the face of tyranny or despotism or fanaticism. In the end, all wars are only one thing: people killing people. This is not to suggest that there cannot be justifiable reasons for responding militarily to acts of aggression that destroy civilian lives. But war in and of itself is ruinous to civilians and must always remain a measure of last resort. It *ought* to be difficult and complex and governed by frustrating processes for achieving global consensus.

The last decade has witnessed an extraordinary if not devastating political appetite for war, made possible by a prevailing belief in its primacy in solving international threats. The rhetoric of "killing scumbags" in Afghanistan and elsewhere has perpetuated a kind of nationalistic fervour in which there is little room for thoughtful dissent, even as the human and financial costs of waging war reach levels that are wholly unsustainable. Annual military spending is now at the highest point since World War II (higher than during the Cold War), with the United States footing half the bill. During his first year in office, President Barack Obama authorized more attacks against suspected terrorists (habeas corpus notwithstanding) by unmanned drones flying over Pakistan than George W. Bush did in his entire presidency. In the process of hitting its targets of armed militants, the Attack of the Drones has also killed civilians, at a ratio of fifty to one. Names and locations of targets are also proposed by the mercurial government of

Pakistan – a military serfdom under whose auspices Osama Bin Laden "hid" for years. No doubt there is some kind of process of intelligence-gathering in place to verify submissions for extrajudicial execution. But "military intelligence," as Groucho Marx once cracked (before Bush rendered it prophecy), "is a contradiction in terms."

In recent years, the rules of war – ranging from how it is fought, to who participates, to what constitutes a legitimate target, to the definition of torture and prisoner of war (frankly, it would be more accurate to say the entire Geneva Convention) – have gone under the knife so many times they are barely recognizable. War profits from our disinterest. And the impossible task of finding out the truth about war – of tracking it from its origins to the depths of human misery – is designed to keep us from thinking critically about war's complexities. This, of course, serves the military's interests, which are inextricably linked to corporate interests, and which are accepted at face value more often than not.

So why care? Well, let's start with the obvious. War is mass murder. Six million Jews. Nearly one million Rwandans. More than five million Congolese. More than one hundred thousand Iraqis. Tens of thousands of Sri Lankans. Three hundred thousand Darfurians. More than seven thousand Allied soldiers in Iraq and Afghanistan. While the *absolute number* of wars declined from forty-one to twenty-five over the past decade, it requires an acrobatic leap of intelligence to declare this a victory for foreign and military policy. Simply counting the number of wars tells us very little about their scale of atrocity or their overall threat to global security. And many countries to have emerged recently from conflict or totalitarian rule are holding on by the thinnest of political and economic threads, placing them only tenuously on the "not at war" side of this equation. Technically, for a war to be counted, there must be one thousand combat-related deaths a year. So, for example, countries flooded with small arms and plagued by roving criminal gangs of non-soldiers – who systematically rape and mutilate young girls but lack identifying uniforms or articulated political objectives – may not be "at war," but neither are they at peace. These kinds of violent elements, common to Haiti, the Democratic Republic of Congo, Sierra Leone, Guinea Bissau, the Ivory Coast, and many other countries, are a major cause of civil unrest and civilian suffering worldwide. And, as too many countries have tragically discovered, some conflicts also have a nasty habit of spilling over borders, toppling governments, and melting into the kind of ideological cesspools from which suicide bombers seep. The war in Afghanistan was a problem long before Al-Qaeda started redecorating the rocky mountain caves of northern Pakistan. Now it is a problem of nuclear proportions. And that's just *one* war.

With billions of dollars in illicit arms traded each year and 15,000 nuclear warheads in the world, it is easy to understand how other people's wars can quickly become our own. But if the untold loss of life and the threat of planetary obliteration cannot rouse us from our domestic bunkers, consider this: war is never as far away as we believe it to be. It is in our pockets, generating annual returns for our pension funds, encircling our ring fingers, and filling up our cars, among other luxuries. This means that, both individually and collectively, we have a far more direct influence over armed conflicts in the world than we might otherwise believe.

Some will dismiss any attempt to dismantle the industry of war as naive, sheltered, ideological thinking. The kind of thinking that will see women stoned to death in soccer stadiums in Kandahar for the "crime" of withholding sex from their husbands, or allow North Korea's Kim Jong-un to run amok in a field of mushroom clouds, or erase the state of Israel from the map. But if there was ever a time for vigorous debate about the balance between war and peace, it is now. And it is long overdue, because the last decade has effectively shut out war's dissenters from public discourse. Those who questioned early on the legitimacy of the 2003 invasion of Iraq were labelled Saddam Hussein sympathizers and maligned as minstrels of tyranny (if you weren't *for* the war, then you must have been *for* Saddam). Those who wondered, out loud, whether a military ante-up in Afghanistan would ever get to the heart of the matter (it did not), and proffered that the money might be better spent on increased development assistance and alternatives to the poppy trade, risked being branded as anti-troop. And yet, I've always found that the courageous men and women sent into battle to do our bidding welcome this kind of open debate, particularly from their governments. It's a tragic shame so little of it has been on offer. We do them a disservice when we assume these aren't the very questions they ask themselves, every day, on the front lines. These are just a few of the false dichotomies we create surrounding war that obstruct reason and help fuel our growing militarization.

I AM A MEDICAL DOCTOR and have worked in and out of war zones over a span of sixteen years, but I'm not the "life saving" kind who reattaches limbs or performs Caesarean sections by candlelight. I'm a public health specialist and a family physician. On the rare occasion when I may have been credited with saving a life, it was only when someone better suited for the task – a trauma surgeon with Médecins Sans Frontières (MSF), perhaps – wasn't available. In keeping with my medical training, my focus in the field has always been on the prevention and containment of threats to people's well-being, hopefully obviating the need for lives to be "saved" as often. To that end, I'm a persistent proponent of investing in the resourcefulness and resilience of local communities, rather than continuously relying on external volunteers and international organizations to fill those critical gaps.

My role has often been to assess local needs, identify risks, propose alternatives, and work with war-ravaged communities to realize their goals for a more peaceful, prosperous, self-reliant society through the establishment of development programs. In some instances I have returned to the same country several times over many years and during different political crises. Throughout my career, I have worked for a mix of academic groups, UN agencies, and non-governmental organizations. I have also co-produced two documentary films on war and have written about the issues confronting civilians in such violent climates for newspapers and magazines. This means that some of the stories featured within this book were the result of journalistic inquiry and had nothing whatsoever to do with the practice of medicine. I have done my best to try to capture many of these experiences in a coherent and unified way to support the book's arguments, without explaining my various roles in each and every case unless this was warranted.

I am a founder of War Child, and for the past eleven years most of my international work has been on behalf of that organization. War Child is an international charity working tirelessly to foster hope and dignity in the lives of children overcoming conflict in some of the most challenging humanitarian environments. What began as an idea in the 1990s to develop a humanitarian organization tasked with bridging the gap between "relief" (as in short-term emergency initiatives concentrating primarily on food, health care, water, and shelter) and "development" programming (longer-term initiatives that normally do not begin until a crisis has ended) to promote social stability in countries wrestling with war has grown into a global initiative. War Child's work overseas targets child and adult education, children's rights, and sexual violence against women and girls, and supports increased economic opportunities for youth. War Child also works to enhance public education and awareness through music and other arts-based initiatives.

When War Child started in North America, there were two other recently formed non-profit entities in Europe called War Child – in the United Kingdom and in Holland – each with its own separate mandate and organizational history. These were independent organizations, despite sharing a common name. This detail is important because my contribution to War Child has been one part of a much larger whole. Over the past couple of years, our three offices have formed a cooperative federation of War Childs in order to share resources and maximize our impact on behalf of children. Collectively, we are now called War Child International (www.warchild.org), with the recent addition of War Child U.S.A., and we work in twenty countries affected by armed conflict.

Some of the criticisms I make in this book may seem antithetical to my own actions and experiences. I *did*, after all, get on a plane bound for Somalia as a volunteer with the United Nations Children's Fund (UNICEF) shortly after completing my medical degree. And I did start yet another humanitarian organization, adding to the glut of entities now clamouring for finite public donations. Without wishing to protest too much on these points, while I am proud to have been a part of War Child's evolution, in no way am I singularly responsible for it. Most significantly, it is War Child's local partners who have built and defined the organization's inclusive approach to field programming, and who continue to be the inspiration. Aid workers, academic experts, human rights lawyers, teachers, artists, employees, community leaders, students, and volunteers in North America and around the world – War Child is the product of *their* courage and tenacity, and I am merely grateful to have witnessed it. And on the question of volunteering overseas and whether that's an appropriate way to "do" relief and development, I've devoted a considerable number of pages in the book to the exploration of this issue, and why it must be approached thoughtfully and carefully. I would not want to discourage anyone from getting involved or choosing humanitarian work, but each of us has a moral obligation to know what we are doing, to be trained and qualified for the task, and to ask hard questions of ourselves.

I did not always appreciate this. My first exposure to the basic idea of humanitarian assistance (this may sound familiar to anyone born between 1965 and 1975) was Live Aid in the 1980s. Bob Geldof's concert for the Ethiopian famine drew 1.5 billion viewers and raised over $140 million.* Moved by the images of Ethiopian children, their skin stretched tightly over their skeletal frames, students at my high school in Toronto held a fundraiser that I enthusiastically took part in. When I think back now, it was the stuff of parodic splendour: we tried to break the record for the world's longest ice cream sundae,

---

* For simplicity, Canadian references are in Canadian dollars. All other amounts are in United States dollars unless otherwise specified.

which we served up in continuous rows in the gymnasium, handing out spoons to anyone who made a donation. As a teenager, I played nothing but "Do They Know It's Christmas?" on my portable boombox from the moment my parents packed away the jaw-destroying Hallowe'en Tootsie Rolls well into spring – to the point where everyone else in the Nutthouse no doubt wished we could skip the Yuletide and go straight to Easter. It would be years before I would discover that more than 30 percent of Ethiopians are in fact Muslim, and an even larger percentage are Orthodox Christians who celebrate Christmas in January. A small percentage are Jewish, several thousand of whom emigrated to Israel as refugees during the famine. So no, many of them did not know that it was *our* Christmas, nor did they care.

My goal in writing this book is not to make anyone feel guilty about past contributions to international humanitarian causes (for example, by donating used clothes or books, financing orphanages, or mounting an eat-a-thon for famine victims). My aim is simply to introduce a process of critical reflection concerning our own actions and deeds, and how, collectively, we are so often implicated in horrific acts of violence around the world, while our personal interventions rarely do more than maintain the status quo.

Those struggling to overcome the violence and hardship that ensnare millions around the world every year want what we all want: dignity in life. They want to see their children grow and thrive, and to not someday find themselves weeping over their bullet-ridden bodies or watching helplessly as they starve to death. From a distance, war is distilled down to geopolitical realities and strategies. But up close, war is personal. It is grandparents gassed to death at Auschwitz. Afghan fathers wrongfully arrested and handed over by NATO forces to be tortured. Little Congolese girls raped until their uteruses rupture and left to bleed to death at the side of the road. An only son who picks up a tiny canister in Iraq believing it might be a toy, only to have it explode in his hands. An abducted Ugandan child soldier made to cut the throat of his younger sister as punishment for attempting to flee. A Canadian recruit on her first tour of duty, returned home to her mother in a body bag. The human dimension of war is always more sobering. And when you've been touched by it, you simply cannot turn your back on it.

Every war zone I have ever worked in has taught me something. Some of these experiences made me angry. Others made me laugh. Many reduced me to tears. And a few filled me with intense regret about the things I might have done differently. These experiences make me neither better nor worse than anyone else – just slightly more adrift, straddling chaos and misery on the one hand, and peace and privilege on the other. It seems odd to have found myself drawn to war zones over the years; to find emotional shelter in the way war reduces existential doubts down to simple truths about the will to survive. But war is surprisingly full of ironies. The chain-smoking nine-year-old rifling through luggage at a nondescript checkpoint in the bush, armed with a Kalashnikov rifle and demanding a copy of *Harry Potter*. The frustrated American soldier shouting, "Don't you want freedom and democracy?" from the top of an armoured security vehicle at a bunch of misanthropic, rock-throwing street children in Karbala, Iraq. The Afghan women who remove their burqas and then proceed to have the kind of intimate conversations that would be too bold even for *Sex and the City* writers. The experience of war shatters all assumptions about who and what we are as human beings – the horrors we are capable of, our ignorance and prejudices, and our ability to show great compassion and courage in the face of extreme adversity. And perhaps this is war's greatest irony: it offers the ultimate perspective on the sanctity of life.

War changes everyone and everything it touches. I am not the same person who boarded a plane for Somalia sixteen years ago, armed with good intentions and bound for a career in international humanitarian relief. I left feeling potentially useful. I returned feeling utterly useless. But it set me on a journey to try to figure out what I *could* do, and this book captures many of those experiences. By understanding how we are a part of war, as people occupying this shared space, we may come to terms with what is needed if we are ever to put a stop to it.

War is not so entrenched that it cannot be undone. I truly believe this. And I hope, after reading this, that others will too.

CHAPTER 1

AN INVITATION TO WAR

There are certain rules about a war, and rule number one
is that young men die. And rule number two is,
doctors can't change rule number one.
COL. HENRY BLAKE TO HAWKEYE PIERCE, M★A★S★H

Goats, burned out cars, and a few spindly acacia trees inter-
rupting an expanse of copper sand: this was what the
landing strip outside Baidoa, Somalia, looked like from 3,000
metres in 1995. Baidoa: the City of Death, where three years
earlier 300,000 people succumbed to starvation and disease.
Now, a new wave of famine was failing to rouse any degree of
outside interest.

Our small, six-seater World Food Programme (WFP) plane
circled above the city once, twice, then a third time, making
sure a handful of children had time to clear our path of valuable
livestock. I was twenty-five years old, had recently finished
medical school, and was midway through a master's program
at the London School of Hygiene and Tropical Medicine.
Somalia – specifically, what happens to the health of women
and girls when states fail – was the subject of my forthcoming
thesis, and I'd signed on as a field volunteer with UNICEF. I'd
met the director of UNICEF Somalia, Pierce Gerety, a few
months prior in Nairobi and had been invited to participate in

a country-wide review of the agency's humanitarian activities. Our maternal and child health assessment would be used for program planning and form the basis of a global appeal.

The UNICEF team knew that the humanitarian situation across the country in 1995 was serious. They needed to know *how* serious, and where to invest their dwindling resources. These are the perplexing questions that international aid agencies face all the time: stay or go, gear up or gear down, vaccinate or chlorinate?

Pierce was an unflinching, charismatic American lawyer in his fifties who'd trained at Yale but ended up eschewing corporate life in favour of tours of duty in the world's hell holes with the United Nations. (Pierce and I would cross paths again several times in different war zones before he lost his life in the Swissair crash off Peggy's Cove, Nova Scotia, in 1998.) I was under contract – so I would be covered by the UN's evacuation order, should one be necessary – for precisely one dollar. The night before my departure for Somalia, I'd joked with Pierce that I was happy to accept the terms of our agreement, but expected to be paid half the money up front. The morning of our flight, he slipped me two quarters and a copy of Efua Dorkenoo's book *Cutting the Rose*, about female genital mutilation. This barbaric ritual is common throughout the world, and particularly widespread in Somalia.

As we prepared to land, I buried the book deep in my knapsack, threw on my standard-issue flak jacket and helmet, and watched as the desiccated remains of this nomadic trading town claimed the horizon.

The first thing about Somalia to confront visitors is the heat. It beats down from above and radiates back from below, turning foreign cheeks a blistering crimson and making the simple act of breathing an effort. (Many of my African friends who came to

Canada as refugees felt the same way about the bitter cold the first time it hit them.) And then there is the smell. It is not the smell of the tropics, of plantains and corn grilling at the side of the road, palm oil and sweet, salted air. In places like Somalia and other countries under siege, it is the stench of rancid, burning garbage, rotting animal corpses, putrid water, and suppurating wounds: the smell of a civilization in decay.

The journey from Baidoa's landing strip (no one would presume to call it an airport) to the centre of the city was eerily dystopian. Gangs of disaffected young men armed with rocket launchers and Kalashnikov rifles owned the streets from the backs of their rusted-out Toyota Hiluxes. The vehicles still displayed the faded logos of the international agencies from which they'd been looted, made available for hire to "internationals" at extortionate rates. Any amount of time spent sitting in the back seat of a diesel-choked vehicle driven by the same vulgar asshole who expropriated it from your predecessor (at gunpoint, no less) while you pay $350 a day for the privilege is a sobering experience.

If I'd arrived in Somalia with a degree of self-righteousness, it faded within minutes of landing, when a grenade (fortunately with its firing pin still firmly attached) rolled under my feet the first time our vehicle came to a stop. When I protested that munitions were not allowed in United Nations vehicles, the driver was quick to point out that the car no longer belonged to the UN, but I was welcome to walk to my destination (which, by any measure of UN security policy, was ill-advised). Being escorted around town by a moonlighting arms trafficker did not quite fit with the role I'd imagined for myself. I was therefore not surprised to learn that during the preceding year many humanitarian agencies and aid workers operating in Somalia had concluded that they no longer had the stomach for it. Their numbers had dropped precipitously, from a peak of nearly two hundred international organizations in 1992 down to forty when I arrived in early 1995. And aid agencies discomforted by Somalia's many compromises needed only to look to the recent Rwandan genocide for a morally defensible "exit strategy."

I arrived in Somalia, like so many aid workers before me, believing I possessed skills that might be of some use. "This is what I am trained to do. This is why I went into medicine," I'd told myself on my departure day, as I wrote "Having a great time!" on the backs of postcards featuring hippos and giraffes at Jomo Kenyatta International Airport in Nairobi before boarding the plane. I postdated them and paid the saleswoman a few extra shillings to mail one every week to my parents in Toronto, who believed I was off on a Kenyan safari and *not* on a flight into one of the world's most dangerous places.* It was a choice that I'd made at an age when I was old enough for it to be an informed one, but still green enough to have my doubts.

Why did I head into a war zone? "Aid worker" seemed to be a logical career path for a committed humanities student who had nevertheless gone on to become a doctor (although I cannot pretend that it all makes sense to me now, even years later). I was unsettled by the human condition. I'd marched against South African apartheid as an undergraduate at McMaster University, attended peace vigils during the 1991 Gulf War, and identified health and human rights as my primary area of interest in my application to medical school. Worldwide, the single greatest impediment to peace, as I saw it then and do now, was the marginalization of women and girls, underlying absurdly high levels

---

* Because that's what I told them. As a parent myself now, I can appreciate what a shameful, awful lie this was.

of maternal, child, and infant mortality across Africa, Asia, and parts of the Middle East. Somalia has had, for the better part of two decades, one of the highest death rates for women during childbirth in the world. I would therefore describe my involvement in the humanitarian dimension of war less as a calling and more as a collision: once the wheels were in motion, the impact was unavoidable.

It took only one afternoon in Baidoa for me to realize that I wouldn't be saving any lives in Somalia: UNICEF was overwhelmed, underfunded, and barely operational in a security climate that required us to travel with armed escorts high on qaat.* My job included visiting UNICEF-supported feeding clinics to interview women about their health and collect data to calculate malnutrition rates. Not the kind of heady stuff that earns doctors their bragging rights in war zones, but necessary for proper program planning. I'd developed a series of standard questions, which my translator, Hawa, dutifully read to the women standing in line as I scribbled down their answers in my journal. The women, mostly younger than me, wore loose, bright wraps and clung to tiny, sallow infants with protruding bellies – too malnourished to cry. As they waited for their children to be seen, the women spoke to me of being incapacitated by malaria, and of being so famished and anemic that their breast milk had run dry. They talked about their husbands, sons, and brothers lost to war, and of their country plagued by violence.

The noonday sun was reaching its apex and I felt light-headed. I moved towards the women at the front of the line, to an area shaded by the clinic's canopy. I could see their babies more closely now. I reached down and placed my index finger in the

---

* Qaat is a leafy narcotic similar to amphetamine.

palm of a small, six-month-old girl cocooned to her mother, who was next in the queue. The baby's taut fingers were cool, her chest motionless. Dead.

My mind reeled. When had she died? While I was asking her mother inane questions about what she needed? What she needed was for her daughter to have a chance at life. Was the baby dead when I arrived and I just hadn't noticed? How could I not notice? Suddenly, any confidence I'd had about my usefulness in the face of such misery was displaced by a sense of ineffectuality.

I looked to Hawa and asked whether she thought the mother knew her baby was dead. Hawa pressed her tongue against her front teeth and forced the air out through her lips, making a *tsk* sound. "She probably know, but maybe she don't accept. And where else can she go?" As I moved my hand away from the baby, unsure what to do next, the young woman turned to speak to Hawa. I knew then by the listless tone in her voice and her gaunt, agonized expression that she understood it was too late for her child.

"She say six months ago," Hawa translated, "after her daughter was born, her husband and her brothers leave her village to fight in the war. Her sisters bring food and collect water. Then road become unsafe. Too many guns. Boys, they shoot and kill people. They rape women. Everyone must stay home. Her animals get sick. She hungry and have no milk for baby. She feed her water and sugar. Baby get sick. She know her baby need help, but too many soldiers to travel to clinic, what can she do? The elders send message to her husband and brothers. No one come. After three weeks, her uncle trade animals for ride in truck for her and baby to get treatment. They drive at night. She held two days at checkpoint: no food, no water. Now she here, but the men that brought her say she must pay more or they won't take her back.

She have no money. She very worried. She have two other children at home."

And so it went in Somalia. A young mother, stranded, clutching her dead baby, with two more children somewhere awaiting the same fate.

"Hawa, please tell her I am sorry." Sorry I couldn't do anything for her. Sorry there was no money to help her bury her child. Sorry I couldn't pay for her ride home, or ask my driver to take her. It was against UN policy, and even if it wasn't, he was unlikely to do me any favours. Sorry that her husband and brothers were most likely dead. Sorry we didn't have the funding to open a clinic closer to her village so that other women could get the care they needed. Sorry that this clinic, too, would soon phase out its operations and close within a few months.

The clinic's intake nurse appeared, dressed in navy mechanic's coveralls. After scanning the names in his spiral-bound book, he took a pen and ruler from his breast pocket and began to draw new columns in the empty pages. Behind him, a torn UNICEF poster touted the benefits of vaccination. Hawa motioned for me to collect my things. I watched as the nurse wrote numbers in the left-hand margin where he compiled the weekly data of those waiting to be seen: "402, 403, 404 . . ." The line snaked around the supplementary feeding tents. Dozens more had arrived in the past hour. The women stood with their mottled, swollen feet pressed into the hot sand, ritually fanning the flies from their children's drawn mouths. The intake nurse asked whether I'd managed to get all the information I needed. "The first woman in line over there," I reported. "Her baby is dead." He returned to his entries: "405, 406, 407." Without looking at me, he said, "Doctor, if you go up to all the women standing in this line, you will find many more dead children." With that, he ushered the young mother and her baby into the assessment room, sat her down, and lifted the lifeless infant onto a wooden exam table.

Sorry. Sorry. Sorry.

In the face of Somalia's insatiable violence, this was what humanitarian interventions had been reduced to: a pathetic apology for the business of war as usual. With every passing day, I increasingly felt as if I was implicated in a lie, propagating the myth of humanitarian aid as a noble response to an ignoble act. In reality, we weren't saving Somalis from themselves, but from failed experiments in development and foreign policy.

Understanding the quagmire that Somalia became – and remains – requires some context. Somalia's current iteration as a failed state began in 1991, the year in which it gave up all pretense of government. Siad Barre, a quasi-socialist dictator installed after leading a bloodless military coup against the elected government in 1969, was forced out of office and fled into exile in Nigeria. Various local warlords viewed Barre's departure as an open invitation to seize control, manipulating Somalia's clan-based allegiances to wage a violent, sadistic war. By 1992, Somalia's capital, Mogadishu, had been reconstituted as the war's front line, cutting off all ports and roads in and out of the city and shutting down the trade routes upon which the country's nomadic civilians depended. Famine is a political failure, one that does not occur in countries with a democratically elected and responsive government and a reasonably free press.

Later that same year, images of skeletal Somali children began streaming across America's news stations as aid agencies struggled to manoeuvre in Somalia's hostile security environment. On December 9, with much fanfare, night-vision cameras captured the dramatic arrival of U.S. Marines (commando style) on the beaches of Mogadishu. Although the United States originally expressed reservations about expanding food aid in Somalia, it became the largest donor of humanitarian assistance to the country. In total, 37,000 international troops were deployed to Somalia in a United Nations–sanctioned, United States–led operation tasked with guaranteeing the safe delivery of humanitarian aid, piously entitled "Operation Restore Hope." While experts argued that the intervention was too late to be useful and risked undermining the tenuous gains being made on the ground to distribute food and disarm local militias, there was another useful reason to stay the course: NATO countries were looking to repurpose their militaries, whose relevance was rapidly collapsing at the end of the Cold War.

Within a month of the first U.S. Marines landing on the beaches of Mogadishu, Bill Clinton was sworn in as the forty-second president of the United States. Clinton needed no convincing on Somalia, declaring that "only the United States could help stop one of the great human tragedies of this time." It was a felicitous mission for America's new Commander in Chief. A war protester during Vietnam, Clinton lacked the "read my lips" combat swagger of his predecessor, George H.W. Bush. But America's first baby boomer president embraced the humanitarian spin on the use of force, and Somalia became his poster child. Under Chapter VII of its Charter, the United Nations had authorized the use of "all necessary means" to ensure the delivery of humanitarian aid in Somalia, with more than twenty countries contributing military personnel to the mission.

As these things go, American forces were not content to stand around protecting high-protein biscuits. Professionally trained militaries have a habit of wanting to kick some proverbial enemy ass, and Somalia had more than its share of bad guys who needed a good, old-fashioned ass-kicking. In particular, one of its most callous presidential aspirants, Mohamed Farrah Aidid, former chief of intelligence to Siad Barre, resented the moralizing strangers impeding his siege of Mogadishu. On June 5, 1993, Aidid launched an attack against UN Pakistani peacekeeping forces, killing twenty-five and wounding another fifty. The blue helmets came off. George Stephanopoulos recounts Clinton's reaction: "With his face reddening, his voice rising, and his fist pounding his thigh, he leaned into Tony (his National Security Advisor, Anthony Lake), as if it was his fault. 'I believe in killing people who try to hurt you. And I can't believe we're being pushed around by those two-bit pricks.'"

And so began the mission creep that pitted the "ungrateful Skinnies" against the foreign crusaders, culminating that October in the downing of two Black Hawk helicopters and the deaths of eighteen American soldiers. Somalia also proved to be disastrous to Canada's peacekeeping reputation after Canadian soldiers tortured and beat to death a Somali teen, Shidane Arone, and then posed for photos with his bloodied body – sick souvenirs of the kill.

The hybrid military-humanitarian forces' inaugural voyage had veered dangerously off course.[*] Canadian and American troops went home, mission unaccomplished, to face cuts to their defence budgets and growing public doubts about their relevance in a post–Cold War, new world order. For aid agencies on the ground in Somalia dealing with the aftermath of the withdrawal, the stubborn image of foreign soldiers storming the beaches of

---

[*] Somalia so plagued Clinton that he made the entirely wrong choice to dig in his heels over deployment to Rwanda, for which he later offered an apology in Kigali in 2005.

Mogadishu brandishing the latest American artillery under a relief banner had damaged local relations. The long-held tenets of aid agencies – that they are an unarmed, peaceful, civilian operation not beholden to any particular party to conflict – had been permanently compromised. From that point forward, anyone claiming he or she was in Somalia to "help" was considered fair game by recalcitrant militias laying claim to the country. By the time I arrived in Somalia, the relationship between Somalis and foreign aid workers, and Somalis and the West more generally, was dominated by one distinct emotion: contempt.

The first piece of advice I was given in Somalia, querulously delivered by a veteran United Nations employee, no less, was, "If you have any business to do with a Somali man, do it before noon. After that they're all strung out on qaat and will be more inclined to shoot you." The day of my arrival in Baidoa, during my briefing by UNICEF's local director, an enigmatic Belgian man named Jean, there was a "mayday" call on his portable radio. It was a representative from CARE International, whose own security guards had surrounded the CARE compound and were blocking staff from leaving until they received additional payment. Heavy gunfire could be heard over the radio throughout his transmissions. My distress must have been obvious, because Jean chuckled and said, "Welcome to Somalia." As it turned out, this was not an unusual occurrence. My meetings with international aid agencies were routinely cancelled because one or more armed individuals had barged into the organization's compound, off-loaded several rounds of ammunition, and were demanding equipment, or the use of the car, or a salary increase, or whatever else they could avail themselves of. In the context of what Somalis themselves were experiencing on a daily basis – violence, threats, intimidation, rape, and paralytic despair – the coarseness of these kinds of interactions between the "aid community," as it is awkwardly called, and their stakeholders seems hardly worth mentioning. My point here is that when the world's militaries rebrand themselves as humanitarian agents rather than strategic operatives acting at the behest of their governments, there is a sense that the business of saving lives is no longer distinct from the business of taking them. For humanitarian assistance to work and to reach those in greatest need, aid workers require a neutral, protected space within which to operate. In that sense, Somalia was a devastating turning point for the humanitarian movement. (I'll come back to this in Chapter 3.)

The dilemma in Somalia wasn't how to slow the tide of death, starvation, and disease. That task wasn't terribly complicated: vaccinate priority groups, chlorinate the drinking water, and set up a short-term food distribution program. The real dilemma was that none of this was possible in the face of drug-hazed, irascible young men armed with automatic rifles who sabotaged progress at every turn. As aid workers, we could chronicle the absurdity of it all, but we could do precious little to stop it. The needs of Somali civilians no longer mattered – not to the war criminals squabbling over vast expanses of non-arable land, not to the foreign press, and not to international heads of state. Most significantly, in the months after the Rwandan genocide and with foreign soldiers under attack in Somalia, western sympathies began to wane. Convinced that its good intentions had been spurned by a bunch of gun-slinging, illiterate goat herders, the public shifted its attention to the former Yugoslavia, where a militarized humanitarian intervention force would be resurrected in Kosovo under the aegis of NATO (after failing to win UN Security Council approval for the mission).

Two decades later, Somalia is no better off. It is still a place of abject poverty, rampant lawlessness, and religious edicts, where little girls have their genitalia hacked off by razor blades in dank rooms, pregnant women double as gun runners, and weapons are the most versatile form of currency. Until recently, when Somalia made the news, it was not about dead babies or starving children, though their numbers remained high. It was about trade routes to the "oiligarchies," militant strongholds, Al-Qaeda training camps, wanton pirates in the Gulf of Aden, and kidnapped foreigners. Security interests trumped humanitarian and development concerns. NATO's role was permanently reshaped by the "war on terror," and enemy ass-kicking is once again "in."

There are many ways to explain away Somalia and its profligate cousins, including Iraq, Afghanistan, Sri Lanka, Libya, Iran, the Democratic Republic of Congo, Sudan, North Korea, Burma, Yemen, the Central African Republic, Chad, and the many other troubled regions where collective suffering has been the de facto state of being. Like Somalia, many are still mired in the effluent of Cold War misadventure and colonial buffoonery. Many are highly ethnicized environments, where tribal or religious affiliations run deep and where scores are often settled over centuries. Far too many of them contain dissident groups of misogynistic sociopaths (the Taliban, the Janjaweed, and the Interahamwe come to mind) who may never be held to account. And it's also the case that many are countries whose governments – and I use that term loosely – can be highly resistant to any inter-national olive branch, especially if it arrives gift-wrapped with a humanitarian bow. Populations living within such environments appear to be locked in a chronic cycle of violence, poverty, and despair, most of which would seem to be outside of their control. But this is an illusion, one that is driven by the assumption that civilians are, both individually and collectively, powerless to prevent war or to make changes in favour of peace.

Over the past decade, the dominant approach to combating the threat of war and extremism has been a military one. Annual worldwide military spending now exceeds $1.7 trillion ($230 per year for every living person), the highest level in forty years. It's a staggeringly large sum of money, unaffordable in any economic context. And yet despite this investment in advanced weaponry, professionally trained militaries, intelligence agencies, and expanded capabilities, terrorism remains stubbornly impervious to western military intervention. Terrorist attacks increased by more than 600 percent between 2001 and 2016, murdering and traumatizing civilians from Mumbai to Manchester, London, Paris, Brussels, New York, Baghdad, Orlando, Boston, to name a few. And while it may be imprudent to measure the return on investment when it comes to military spending based on terrorism rates alone (which are influenced by a number of variables), it is reasonable to deduce that this is not a situation where might alone is capable of making right. What, then, are the alternatives?

Much of the answer lies in understanding how dissident groups living in impoverished, combustible countries gain easy access to weapons. The most rapidly expanding weapons market is in developing countries, which currently account for more than 80 percent of all global arms-transfer agreements. It would be comforting to believe that these transfers are restricted to stable democracies in developing countries, ones in which the government is seeking to protect rather than attack its own people: And such a policy would certainly be prudent. But this is not an industry driven by ethics, nor is it one that allows future security risks to trump short-term financial returns. All too often, weapons transfers are approved to highly questionable authoritarian regimes, or the arms end up being resold through illegal channels. In 2009, for example, the government of Sri Lanka borrowed $300 million from Russia to buy arms as it escalated its military offensive against the Tamil Tigers (LTTE). During the three years prior to the end of their decades-long civil war, Britain and other European Union countries, as well as the United States (which suspended sales only in 2008), approved exports of tens of millions of dollars' worth of arms and military equipment to Sri Lanka. Between 20,000 and 40,000 Sri Lankan civilians were killed in the final months of the war. Both the LTTE and the Sri Lankan government are accused of committing war crimes and crimes against humanity during the final stages of the conflict.

In Sudan, China and Iran continued supplying Sudanese president Omar al-Bashir with arms even as the corpses piled ever higher in Darfur. In recent years, the combined arms sales of the top one hundred arms-producing companies in the world have soared to over $375 billion in 2016 – a 40 percent increase since 2002. The biggest and most troubling growth has been in the small arms or light weapons market. This includes assault rifles, machine guns, mortars, rocket-propelled and hand grenades – the preferred arsenal of petty miscreants with an axe to grind.

Every year, 8 million rocket launchers, shoulder-fired missiles, assault rifles, grenades, and machine guns are added to the 900 million or so already in circulation. Some of these end up in the hands of legitimate armies and police forces around the world, but far too many of them do not. This is hardly surprising, given that the black-market price of an assault rifle in a war-torn country averages less than the price of admission to an American theme park. Furthermore, the unwillingness of many arms-producing countries to disclose information related to the sale or transfer of arms and munitions deliberately frustrates the task of holding governments accountable. Canada, which is among the world's top twenty arms exporters, has had one of the lowest international Arms Transparency ratings among industrialized economies – marginally better than Russia's.

With many of the world's major arms exporters openly flouting even the most basic measures of accountability, it is little wonder that other arms-producing countries see no point in even pretending to exercise due diligence. To that end, while the United States remains the world's top arms exporter, accounting for slightly more than 30 percent of world sales, less is known about China's and Russia's arms-producing enterprises, which benefit from state-sanctioned secrecy. China doesn't produce reliable data on its weapons sales, making it impossible to accurately measure the value of its military exports, which is estimated to be in the billions of dollars. This lack of rigour surrounding the arms trade – from the point of manufacturing, through to government export controls, to a shipment's arrival on a combustible foreign shore – ensures that the arms industry is proffered every conceivable market advantage. It is an industry with very few consistently applied global mechanisms of accountability. And a weapon such as the AK-47 is virtually indestructible, guaranteeing that once in circulation its first stop will never be its last. The biggest problem with all of this – well known to anyone who has been on the receiving end of a glabrous teenager armed with an AK-47 and a callous disregard for human life – is that this availability of cheap weapons in fragile, impoverished states is an invitation to war. Even Mikhail Kalashnikov has expressed regret that he did not invent a lawn mower instead.

The flip side to any argument for tighter restrictions surrounding the manufacturing and transfer of weapons (one favoured by those who take a cold-dead-hands approach to arms control) is that if people want to kill people, they'll find a way to do it. But given that people often *do* want to kill people, particularly in places where there are relatively few repercussions for doing so, why entice them with hundreds of rounds per minute of firepower? Civil liberties activists are also quick to decry efforts to restrict the global sale or transfer of arms, citing resistance movements such as the African National Congress, which led to the toppling of apartheid in South Africa, and Paul Kagame's armed rebel movement in Rwanda, which brought about an end to the 1994 genocide. Who will defend the disenfranchised against tyrannical despots such as Robert Mugabe and Moammar Gadhafi? In reality, such trite rationalizations have little bearing on the current conflict environment, where many self-declared revolutionaries are nothing more than profiteers and war criminals. These modern-day "revolutionaries" have included Joseph Kony, northern Uganda's self-proclaimed prophet, who has abducted tens of thousands into his child army; Foday Sankoh, leader of Sierra Leone's Revolutionary United Front, who amputated the hands, ears, and legs of civilians during that country's bloody civil war; Laurent Kabila, whose siege of the former Zaire left a trail of millions of corpses; and Charles Taylor, who brutalized Liberian civilians for nearly two decades while wooing supermodels with his ill-gotten gains.* Even the Taliban in Afghanistan still consider themselves to be righteous defenders of an Islamic movement under siege. Pro-democracy movements in the Arab

---

* Naomi Campbell, testifying during Taylor's war crimes tribunal, claimed that, before meeting him at a 1997 dinner, she had never heard of Mr. Taylor or of Liberia. She was, at the time, being deposed about the conflict diamonds he was alleged to have given her after dinner one evening.

world in early 2011 raised similar questions about whether to arm opposition movements. But as proved to be the case during the Syrian conflict, such proxy wars are bloody and yield dubious outcomes, particularly in regions with pronounced ethnic and religious divisions.

While the notion of guerilla-styled freedom fighters retains populist appeal, the true revolutionaries of our time are the dogged local journalists, women's organizations, and human rights defenders who are routinely harassed, imprisoned, or killed for their progressive ideas. They seek solidarity and the ongoing resources to do their jobs, yet the current ratio of defence to development spending disfavours them.

In 2010, Canada's Conservative government froze Official Development Assistance at $5 billion a year for five years. It was the largest of all government cutbacks in its deficit-trimming budget. Within a few months, Prime Minister Stephen Harper had announced a $9 billion purchase of F-35 American fighter jets. The Parliamentary Budget Office later revised this projection, concluding that the real cost of the jets, once maintenance was factored in, would be closer to $30 billion. It's a worrisome pattern: American government-to-government military sales alone have tripled over the past decade, including shipments to the perennially oppressive House of Saud, which in turn provided military support to autocrats in Bahrain as they crushed protesters during the 2011 "Arab Spring," and which has been actively involved in an ongoing and lethal war in Yemen. In the months before Muammar Gadhafi's overthrow following the Libyan revolt, the Pentagon had entered into negotiations with the now deceased despot to develop bilateral military ties and to deliver armoured troop carriers worth $77 million. And why shouldn't they? In the five years after the 2004 embargo against

Gadhafi was lifted, the European Union approved licences worth over $1 billion in arms exports to Libya. A few years later, many of these same NATO countries spent hundreds of millions of dollars on a military intervention which ultimately plunged the already fragile country into chaos and emboldening terror and other militant groups across in Libya, Syria, Mali and beyond.

Military spending among NATO countries *and* developing countries has risen sharply over the past decade. Among the world's poorest countries, education expenditures as a share of their Gross Domestic Product (GDP) are lower than military expenditures. It is hard to believe that any country will be better served in the years to come by a less-educated, more-militarized populace. And who is profiting from this trend? Let's start with North America's teachers.

In Canada, at least seven out of ten provincial teachers' pension funds hold more than $2.7 billion in investments in the world's top one hundred arms manufacturers. Two – Nova Scotia and Newfoundland – also may have investments in arms manufacturers but have been unwilling to disclose this information. However, despite repeated requests to these bodies to disclose this information over more than a year, they had still not provided their list of holdings by the time of publication. Leading the pack for the past few years has been the Ontario Teachers' Pension Plan, representing 284,000 of Ontario's active and retired school teachers. At the start of 2010, Ontario's teachers' pension fund held over $90 million in investments in Lockheed Martin, the world's largest military producer. The same is true in the United States. In 2016 the New York State and California State Teachers' Retirement Systems alone had $1.7 and $3 billion invested in weapons manufacturers. When teachers start betting on a boom in weapons sales to see them through their golden years, it's time to load the trunk of the car with flashlights and soup cans.

The growing profitability of the arms industry has not gone unnoticed by fund managers more generally. The Canada Pension Plan (CPP), to which every Canadian earning a paycheque must contribute, holds in excess of $1 billion in investments in thirty-seven of the world's top one hundred arms-producing companies. I could easily fill the next one hundred pages of this book with the ominous holdings of some of North America's most respected investment plans, but it would only be restating the obvious: we are consumers of war.

The week before I was set to leave Somalia, our team flew to Bosasso, a city on the Gulf of Aden, the gateway to the Middle East. In the evenings before curfew, I occasionally ventured out to swim, fully clothed, in the shallow waves that crested just beyond Bosasso's ragged shores. A guard stood by, shaking his head at my foreign insouciance and needling me to be mindful of the sharks that had "eaten their fill of dead Somalis." It was a luxury to be freed from Somalia's relentless dust and oppressive chaos.

One morning, having opted out of yet another interminable inventory of health clinic stock rooms, I asked the UNICEF driver to take me to the resettlement camps housing those displaced by the violence in Somalia's rural areas. I told the team I would meet up with them later in the afternoon. A cholera epidemic was reportedly surging in the area, and families had been seen digging shallow graves for their children in the parched earth. By spending an afternoon interviewing women in the camps, I hoped to get a better understanding of the prevention strategies that UNICEF could implement and how many would likely be affected. With hospitals in the north struggling to offer patients anything more than condolences, I failed to see the point of continuing to admit people, only to send them home to dengue, malaria, dysentery, or some other life-threatening illness that needed to be interrupted at its source.

The driver dropped me and my translator at the edge of town, where shelters made from plastic sheeting and corrugated metal protruded between emaciated livestock, the blackened remains of cooking fires, and open pits of garbage and feces. "These camps are managed privately," my translator cautioned, struggling to navigate the terrain in her heeled plastic sandals. "The UN has no authority to change anything here." As an educated Somali with a respectable job, she believed in helping those with better odds. She'd been writing to distant relatives in North America and the Gulf States, pleading with them to sponsor her refugee applications. "I have a cousin in Toronto," she'd told me over lunch. "Can you please take a photo of me and send it to him with this letter?" She passed me a note written in English on sheer, ironed stationery, in schoolgirl calligraphy.

"Let's start with this woman," I proposed, waving to a mother fanning her infant behind a half-drawn jute curtain stitched together from World Food Programme bags. The young woman nodded for me to approach. The one-room space, less than fifty square feet, was hot and dark, with a ceiling too low to allow us to stand. "We are normally six," she explained. "Two of my children have gone to collect firewood. The youngest are in town, begging for food." Her baby had the distinctly etiolated look of malaria.

We moved from squat to squat, asking the women where they collected water, where they found food, where their families went to the bathroom, whether any aid agencies had visited them, whether they knew children who had died from watery diarrhea. Their answers were consistent: The women travelled three kilometres, often more, to town every day to collect water from a stagnant creek. Their children all had some form of diarrhea. The women defecated outside, wherever it was private, but the children would go anywhere. One aid agency had come by, many months ago. They'd built a drinking water reservoir in the centre of the camp, and it was filled regularly. *Something was wrong.* Why would the women walk several kilometres for water, and why was the mortality rate from cholera *increasing*, if an aid agency was providing the camp with clean drinking water? No one seemed to know. One elderly woman suggested it was because the more distant water from town "tastes sweeter." It was hard not to scream, "That's because there's shit in it!"

I asked the women to show me the camp water reservoir. They pointed towards a clearing, but none seemed particularly enthused about accompanying me for an inspection. By this point, my translator had had enough and announced that she was going to find the driver.

I walked deeper into the camp, sidestepping frantic chickens and ducking under clotheslines. The reservoir sat above ground, whitewashed to keep the water cool, with a non-governmental organization (NGO) logo emblazoned on its side in big, bold letters. (There was no risk of this good deed going unnoticed.) I still could not figure out why the women wouldn't use it, especially because the water they were walking farther to collect was most likely responsible for killing many of their children. Then again, in Somalia rumours abound that tetanus vaccinations (because they were only given to women of child-bearing age) were actually a form of sterilization – a "western ploy" to rid the world of Africa's "aggravations." Tetanus was a common enough killer among newborns and was entirely preventable, and still many women refused immunization. With this in mind, I began to wonder if someone had erroneously fingered the reservoir as the source of the diarrheal epidemic, and the women were disinclined to admit this to a foreigner. If so, that would be easy enough to fix: I would call the aid agency responsible and suggest they meet with the camp elders to clear up the confusion.

As I looked around for the vehicle to take me back to the compound, a small child approached the reservoir with a plastic jerry can. Not everyone, it seemed, was afraid to use it. He turned the tap and clear water flowed onto his shorts as he struggled to steady his container. The mud ran red beneath his feet, as it can only in Africa. I smiled at him, walked over to help, and afterwards asked if I could take his picture. He mugged for the camera, proud of his grown-up accomplishment.

As he swung the jerry can onto his shoulder and started home, six young men ran towards me from different directions, screaming and pointing their AK-47s at me. It happened too quickly for me to panic. "I'm sorry, I'm sorry," I said, as I tried to coax them to put down their weapons. "Doctor, doctor, UN," I explained, showing them my ID badge. I was not sure whether this would help or hurt me – if this was a kidnapping, the price of my ransom had just shot up.

The men surrounded me and grabbed my camera. "Open, open!" one yelled, holding my camera case, while the others kept their weapons at the ready. "You take picture? No picture! Open!"

"I took picture, yes, yes. I'm sorry," I replied. I handed everything over: camera, backpack, notes, sunglasses, all of it. "Child with water. No picture allowed?" At this point, stupid was my best option.

The one who appeared to be in charge was not satisfied. I could tell he was high on qaat. His henchmen reeked of sour liquor. "You journalist?"

"No, no journalist. Doctor. Children here in camp very sick. I can help." He clearly didn't believe me.

"You UN?"

"Yes, UN."

"The UN help no one in Somalia."

"I want to help."

"Then leave Somalia."

He turned to his entourage and divided up the spoils of my backpack. I sensed they were unsure of their next move. Every part of me wanted to lash out, to grab one of the Kalashnikovs and shout: "Do you rape the women of this camp at night with these pointed at their children? *This* is killing your country. *This* is all that gives you power." Instead, I tried to look as pathetic as possible, helpless, regretful, deferential. "Please, I'm married. My husband is waiting for me," I lied, hoping it would make me less detestable.

"Your husband," he sneered, "needs to teach you better."

He translated for the others, and they laughed. One jostled his fly. Women know these kinds of men, instinctively. Now I was afraid.

At that moment my UNICEF vehicle tore around the corner and our guards jumped out, training their rifles on the crowd of men. Everyone was yelling, posturing, weapons at the ready. I crouched down with my arms over my head. My driver quickly opened the rear passenger door, grabbed me by the back of the shirt, and pushed me onto the floor of the vehicle. He darted back behind the wheel just as the confrontation became more heated and shots were fired into the air.

I looked up to see my translator on the floor with me. "Keep your head down," she whispered. "Stay low." I could hear the thudding of our guards climbing back onto the truck. One stepped into the back seat, pointing his rifle and shouting through the open window. We took off at high speed, and I could hear more shots. Warning shots? Retaliatory shots? I couldn't tell. A minute later, everything was silent. No one was injured. Our driver stopped and suggested I take a seat for the ride back to the compound.

"I'm sorry for the trouble I caused," I began, but no one cared for a debriefing. The driver radioed the head office that we were returning. I was shaking, but fought the urge to cry, given that everyone else in the car had undoubtedly lived through far worse. My translator seized the opportunity to reprimand me. "Those are not good people in the camps. It is not safe."

The next day, our team pulled up to Bosasso's landing strip for the return voyage to Baidoa and discovered that our World Food Programme plane had been seized by another group of armed young men. One of them was under the plane gripping a mounted machine gun, with an ammunition belt coiled around the landing gear. Our pilot, retired South African military, met us before we stepped out of the car and leaned through the open window. "Right. They are saying Bosasso declared independence from Somalia last night, and they are imposing a new exit tax. It's $300 a person. American dollars only. You want to pay, yes or no? If we don't pay, you may be here a few more days."

We radioed to UNICEF HQ to explain the situation, and one of the staff was sent over to handle negotiations. UNICEF had advised the local leadership that this kind of harassment had to stop or the organization would suspend its programming in the north. They had been reassured that it would: the pall of more dead children was unlikely to improve any warlord's chances of retaining power. After a few hours, our departure was cleared and no *baksheesh* was paid. However, the same armed group later surrounded the UNICEF compound, locking the staff inside for several days as they took potshots at the building.

A short while later in Baidoa, I learned what had triggered the confrontation in the camp. Camp officials eventually confided to UNICEF that the landowner was charging them to access the drinking water, and his armed guards were regularly harassing residents and demanding payment. He justified this extortion by claiming he was not being sufficiently compensated by the UN for the use of his property, which was worth far less now that his tenants had cut down all the trees and littered it with refuse. The landowner had seen me going from tent to tent to interview women, and he suspected that they had complained to me about his scheme. When he saw me take a picture of the boy at the water reservoir, he assumed it was to document their concerns. When confronted, he claimed he'd called on his "personal security guards" to "explain to the young woman that pictures are not authorized in the camp." At least, this is how it was relayed to UN officials.

Peace, development, and security will remain stubbornly out of reach for any civilian population choking on weapons fed to them by countries with eighty times their GDP. That's not to deny the culpability of leaders within war-torn nations who liberally finance militia groups, or fill shipping containers with assault rifles instead of primary school books. But when our national pension funds profit from this social malaise, and when our prevaricating governments – wittingly or not – would rather give a one-fingered salute than open the books on what, precisely, is being shipped to whom, we too become part of a very sinister equation. It's easy to point fingers at the moral degenerates who open fire on a busload of schoolgirls in Afghanistan in the name of some ill-founded religious or political agenda. It's more complex to follow the path of those weapons back to their point of origin and ask what more might have been done to prevent such an atrocity.

The extent of the weapons problem in Somalia thwarted every effort to contain the war and the suffering it caused. Even after an arms embargo was declared in 1992, Ethiopia, Eritrea, Yemen, Egypt, Saudi Arabia, and others continued to ship arms to Somalia's warring factions and religious zealots, who had unfettered access to aggrieved young men. NATO countries, in turn, readily sent arms to many of those on that list. During the 2010 World Cup, Somalia's Islamo-fascist youth brigade, Al-Shabab (which has also managed to capture the imagination of young men from Somalia's North American diaspora), succeeded in blowing up civilian targets in Uganda's capital city, Kampala, killing seventy-six and seriously injuring dozens more. These young men have been raised by war and suckled by religious fanaticism. Al-Qaeda recognizes their disaffection as capital and deploys it strategically to provoke fear and wage war on its enemies. We are fighting the wrong battles while placing pathological bets on our own failures.

Years later, I still think of Somalia as the experience that had the most permanent, psychically shattering impact on me. All of my smug, comfortable, undergraduate assumptions about civil war in Africa – that it stemmed from centuries of exploitation and colonial misjudgment followed by intractable poverty, corrosive Cold War influences, and a corrupted body politic – ceded to a pervading sense of shame and indignation. There is a cost to every commercial transaction, and yet the question so rarely asked when it comes to the sale and transfer of weapons globally is this one: Who pays? In the end, we all do.

CHAPTER 2

CHAOS INCORPORATED

History, despite its wrenching pain, cannot be unlived,
but if faced with courage, need not be lived again.
MAYA ANGELOU

Nadine was efficient: there would be none of the usual
Congolese formalities of thanking God, President Kabila,
or the "heavenly fates" for bringing us together. She was one of
only three girls attending a skills-training program in a dusty
field on the margins of Bukavu, in eastern Democratic Republic
of Congo, close to the Rwandan border. She knocked on the
door of my impromptu office: a white plastic table and two chairs
in a crumbling classroom patterned with bullet holes and secured
by thick metal bars on the windows.

I had spent the morning interviewing a handful of former
child soldiers, whose year-long rehabilitation had left them with
the dim view that life would only improve on their eighteenth
birthday, whereupon they could legally return to the militias
that had surrendered them to the United Nations peacekeeping
authority at the age of fourteen. They missed life in the bush,
and resented the international laws, and their proponents, that
had forced them to abandon it.

It was hard not to see their point: once they'd surrendered
their weapons, most of these children were shuffled off to

disarmament, demobilization, and reintegration (DDR) transit centres, which offered minimal education and psychological support. Then they were sent back into communities often resistant to their return. Finally, the lucky ones were foisted onto skills-training programs that churned out hundreds of electricians, carpenters, and roofers without pausing to wonder how many the market could reasonably absorb. Meanwhile, the prospects for those trained in the art of warfare were infinite.

Nadine was tall, with shorn hair and rounded features. She looked to be in her early twenties, but her awkwardness suggested otherwise. "My teacher told me you work for an organization that helps children in war," she said, easing herself into the room.

"I do," I replied in French. "I'm here collecting information because we'll be starting an education program in a few months for children who missed the chance to go to school. Some of the other youth have been sharing their ideas with me. Maybe I can learn from you? Would you like to sit down?"

She slumped into the cracking chair, folded her hands on her lap, and shuffled her feet restlessly. I opened my notebook, and pulled out my pen. I wondered how I must have looked to her, with my workbooks and bottled water and private space.

"Do people in your country know what's happening here in the Congo?" she asked.

"Some do. But there are many distractions."

"What is your impression of the Congo?"

"I think it is a country with many riches. Riches people fight to control, and which are the source of much suffering."

"We die for things we have never seen, never touched. *On meurt pour rien.*" We die for nothing.

———

FOR CENTURIES, the Congo has persisted as an African nation with a boundless capacity to stoke foreign greed. In the seventeenth century, Portugal began exporting thousands of Congolese as slaves to the Americas. In 1885, King Leopold II of Belgium established the Congo Free State, which he claimed as his own private colony. The Belgians plundered the Congo's rubber plants, leaving a trail of corpses, amputees, and scorched old-wood forests, while Leopold erected grand, gilded palaces and monuments with the spoils.

Congo gained independence from Belgium in 1960 under the leadership of Patrice Lumumba, who became the country's first democratically elected prime minister that June. But less than three months later, Lumumba was deposed in a CIA-sponsored coup and later executed by firing squad. From 1965 until 1997, the Congo (renamed Zaire in 1971) was ruled by Mobutu Sese Seko, who governed just as his colonial predecessors had done: with an extraordinary sense of entitlement. During the thirty-two years that Mobutu lorded over the country, he amassed a personal fortune estimated at $5 billion.

As Mobutu's grip began to loosen in the mid-1990s, refugees from Rwanda spilled across the border into the already fragile eastern provinces of Zaire. Many were fleeing the 1994 genocide, but the exodus also included the architects of the Rwandan slaughter: Hutu extremists who'd perfected the art of anti-civilian warfare. With Mobutu's support, Hutu-led militias then used Zaire as a staging ground to launch cross-border raids into Rwanda, setting off a conflict that finally toppled Mobutu's rotting regime in 1997.

By 1998, the newly renamed Democratic Republic of Congo (DRC) was at the centre of a war that eventually involved nine African countries. The conflict forced millions of Congolese from their homes and villages and spawned a legion of militia groups,* which relied on pubescent boys to wage a bloody war that has left more than 5 million dead. The war in the Congo has earned the regrettable distinction of being the worst war, in terms of the number of civilians killed, since World War II (and the worst in African history).

In 2000, more than 5,000 United Nations peacekeepers were deployed to the Congo to restore peace and security, and ensure that the ceasefire agreement between warring factions was observed. It was an absurdly low number given the massive territory they would be required to cover. The war officially ended with the 2002 signing of the Pretoria Agreement, in which the Congo's assorted militia groups agreed to a power-sharing arrangement. In reality, the signing of the peace accord replaced one ruthless conflict, in which armed groups could at least claim to have a quasi-political agenda, with another, in which lawlessness and anarchy *were* the end game. As long as eastern Congo remained incurably unstable, wealth could continue to flow among the arms dealers, mining companies, smugglers, foreign governments, corrupt officials, itinerant rapists, and war criminals† fully committed to this task.

For many Congolese, life has not improved much since Charles Marlow transported ivory for The Company in Joseph Conrad's

---

* Several militia groups initially coalesced under rebel leader Laurent Kabila, father of current Congolese president Joseph Kabila. Their rampage across the country, with the support of an estimated 10,000 child soldiers, culminated in a coup that toppled Mobutu in the capital, Kinshasa, and installed Laurent Kabila as president in 1997. Kabila was assassinated in January 2001, when he was shot by one of his bodyguards.

† These categories are not mutually exclusive. There is, in fact, far too much overlap.

Heart of Darkness more than a century ago. Perhaps the starkest difference is that the Congo's wealth is no longer principally above ground, but rather within it: in its oleaginous rivers, clay soil, and volcanic rock, in the form of gold, diamonds, tin, copper, tungsten, cobalt, and columbite-tantalite (coltan, for short). Coltan is an ore that yields the metal tantalum, which is one of four minerals mined in eastern Congo used to make capacitors in electronic devices including cell phones, digital cameras, video game consoles, and computers. Between 60 and 80 percent of the world's coltan deposits are in eastern Congo, where it is collected by hand. Production increased by nearly 80 percent between 2010 and 2014. This resource is used in developed countries every day, yet most have no idea what it is or where it comes from.

———

"How old are you, Nadine?"

"Seventeen."

Dressed in her blue batik wrap skirt and stained cream blouse, she had the appearance of someone trapped between neglect and despair. As is the case for many girls Nadine's age, her parents had seen no reason to waste the family's limited resources sending her to school: by the time of their first period, most Congolese girls stay home to help with domestic duties. So I was surprised that Nadine's mother had encouraged her to participate in a skills-training program, particularly one focused on the male-dominated trades of carpentry and construction.

"What do you think of this program?" I asked.

"My mother thinks it will be good for me. She wants me to be able to take care of myself." I was inclined to believe that Nadine's mother wanted what my own mother did: to raise her daughters to have choices she never had. But in the Congo, the real narrative is never what you presume it to be.

Nadine then added, "Because she knows I will never marry."

What came next was a story familiar to many Congolese girls and women. One afternoon, after several months of being ill with malaria, Nadine walked into town to buy medication. She carefully folded the bills her mother had given her and pushed them deep into her skirt pocket.

Walking along the dirt road from her village, Nadine remembered feeling better than she had in a while, though she admitted to being distracted by the money in her pocket. She wondered whether she could convince the pharmacist to add a few sweets to her bag – at least one for the long walk home. The closer she got to town, the more relaxed she felt. There were people everywhere. Schoolgirls, hair teased and pulled into fine braids pinched with bright clips, in their best white blouses and oversized kilts, skipped over murky puddles littered with garbage. Shirtless teenagers filled and refilled potholes with gravel, then flagged down passing cars in search of payment for their "public service." Wiry preadolescent boys smashed large rocks into smaller piles, periodically darting into traffic to load their bounty onto donkey carts. For a young farm girl, it was a confusion of debris, people, bleating animals, plastic bags, and exhaust fumes. When the knife pressed against her throat, she'd been unaware that anyone was behind her.

The young men weren't even as tall as Nadine, nor were they particularly strong, but they were well coordinated. One pulled her by the neck, the blade cutting into her flesh. The other gripped her thighs and tore at her skirt as they dragged her, kicking and wailing, down an embankment. A third waved his machete at onlookers, screaming at them to move along unless they "wanted a turn." As they forced her to the ground she realized, for the first time, that she knew these boys. They were former Mayi-Mayi soldiers from a neighbouring village who'd been demobilized and could often be seen loitering in the local markets.

The Mayi-Mayi are militia groups that terrorized eastern Congo during the war and who have been implicated in egregious human rights violations. They draw recruits by abducting or bribing mostly rural children (or their parents) into their ranks. Some families even believe that offering one or more of their children to this perversion will protect their families from further attack. The Mayi-Mayi, and other rebel groups operating in eastern Congo, are known to amputate the arms, lips, breasts, penises, and ears of civilians in the course of their attacks. They maintain loyalty through a toxic combination of drugs, fear, intimidation, and alienation. The children are also indoctrinated in a bizarre mysticism that leaves them believing they have the power of invisibility and can become impervious to bullets by spraying themselves with "magic water." I was once introduced to a ten-year-old boy named Bonneannée at a transit centre for recently demobilized child soldiers in Bukavu. He claimed to have joined the Mayi-Mayi, voluntarily, at the age of six. While most Mayi-Mayi are boys, thousands of girls have also been abducted and used as porters, cooks, sex slaves, and as "rewards" for top recruiters.

With the knife pressed firmly against her by one assailant while her legs were pried apart by another, they took turns raping Nadine, telling her how lucky she was to have such "brave warriors teach her about sex," and that the other girls in her village would be jealous. They kicked her and beat her as blood and semen trailed down her thighs. When she thought it was over, she tried to run. They grabbed her, punching her breasts and face, then pinned her to the ground. The boy with the knife dug the corroded blade into the heel of her foot, cutting a deep incision as he sliced away at the soles of her feet. As she screamed and struggled, he grabbed the other foot and started over. "Run! Run!" they taunted. Then they raped her again until she lost consciousness.

Nadine slipped her feet out of her worn sneakers and ran her fingers along the ridged scars. "When I awoke, I was alone and naked. A group of school children helped me find my clothes and washed them in a gutter so my mother would not see the blood. I did not want her to know what happened. I could not walk, so they carried me home."

In the Congo, there is very little shame in raping, but there is tremendous shame in being raped. Victims are often derided and forced from their homes and communities. For a girl Nadine's age, the stigma of rape can undermine her prospects for marriage and sentence her to a life of poverty and servitude. HIV prevalence in the Congo nears 25 percent – even higher among combatant groups. Given the violent nature of these assaults, the chances of rape victims becoming infected is high. For these reasons, not only are many Congolese women and girls reluctant to report cases of rape, particularly in the context of an almost non-existent judicial system and a corrupt police force that can be easily suborned by rapists, but they also rarely seek treatment for their injuries. "If I am infected with AIDS, I do not want to know," Nadine told me. "But if my father can find someone who is willing to marry me, I will have to prove that I am clean."

Nadine hadn't told anyone about the multiple rapes, not even her mother. "No, I never told her about it. She put me in the program after one of the militia leaders bragged about my rape to women in the market. He said that some of his boys had really enjoyed me and I'd begged them for more. My mother said I could either ask one of my rapists to make me his bush wife or I would have to learn to take care of myself, because none of the boys in the village would want me now."

A few months after Nadine and I spoke, she was raped again.

The sadistic rape of young girls, infants, mothers, and grand-mothers is pervasive in the Congo. It has become a kind of national rot, decaying families, communities, marriages, and the country's entire social structure. Among those doing the raping are government soldiers, rebel fighters, UN peacekeepers, hus-bands and fathers, and an infinite supply of demobilized, idle young men. The Congo, for all its spotty attempts at democ-racy and governance, peace accords, more than $2.5 billion in annual aid, and a peacekeeping operation that has cost in excess of $10 billion since 1999, has been unable to pull itself from the refuse of war. Instead, it is stuck in a perpetual state of "unwar" – a lawless abyss – the causes of which are at once obvious and complicated to address.

Most of the ongoing conflict in the Congo takes place in the eastern part of the country, in the Kivu provinces, along the border with Rwanda, Burundi, and Uganda. This area is also home to the majority of the country's mines, worth as much as $25 trillion. In 2009, doctors working at Panzi Hospital in Bukavu collected data on violent rape in South Kivu from women who were seeking treatment for horrific injuries. (The term "Rape with Extreme Violence" encompasses gang rape, genital mutilation, insertion of knives or other weapons into a woman's vagina or rectum, and other atrocities.) When they plotted the location of these attacks on a map, they found that cases of rape clustered around mining areas. Based on their findings, it didn't appear to matter who was managing the mines. Whether it was Congolese government forces, Rwandan rebels, Mayi-Mayi, or any other group, it amounted to a wretched maw of sexual predators, youth gangs, corrupt officials, trigger-happy mercenaries, thieves, and war criminals, with easy access to cash, weapons, and drugs, preying on hapless civilians. While rape occurs in other regions of the Congo as well, there's no denying the pronounced and destructive impact of the mining sector on the safety and security of Congolese women and children.

The Congo's resource wealth doesn't just fuel local violence: it's also the source of funding for much of the country's conflict with its neighbours. The Enough Project, a Washington-based NGO and leading international voice on the relationship between resource exploitation and conflict, estimated that in 2008 illicit minerals trading resulted in $185 million flowing to armed groups. This revenue from mineral wealth in the DRC is shared with an assortment of militias inside the Congo and in border states, including Rwanda, Uganda, and Burundi, evidenced by the glaring inconsistencies between national production and export statistics. For example, in 2016, Rwanda is estimated to have earned $90 million from coltan exports (representing 30 percent of the total global market), despite having only a limited domestic production capacity of its own. Meanwhile, Uganda, which domestically produces very little gold, has seen a dramatic surge in gold exports, from $74 million in 2007 to $340 million in 2016, almost all of which was likely derived from mines in the DRC. While it is difficult to know, given the surreptitious nature of the Congo's mining industry, how much of the country's minerals and precious metals are illegally transferred across its borders every year, a 2009 report by the DRC Senate – the most recent one available – estimated it to be in the order of 80 percent. Soldiers at border crossings on all sides have been known to receive kickbacks to ignore rampant smuggling from eastern Congo. And once these mining resources enter Rwanda or Uganda they can be declared "conflict free" and sold into international markets.

The government of Joseph Kabila points to the Congo's resource wealth as essential to the country's recovery. It can supply the financial means to build roads, schools, universities, and hospitals, create jobs, pay public servants, provide electricity, end the Congo's reliance on international aid, and bring the country's infrastructure into the twenty-first century. But this assumes a direct relationship between the revenues generated by government-owned mines and social spending. This relationship simply does not exist. The proportion of recorded taxes collected from the Congo's mining sector is slightly more than one tenth of the total that ought to be generated by the sector based on revenue analyses. And every year, there is at least a billion dollars in revenues from the Congo's mining sector that simply vanishes. Corruption, instability, improper monitoring, and profiteering dominate in the absence of rigid accountability measures. The Congolese government has also refused to enforce international norms in relation to its mining sector. In allowing the rampant use of child labour and ignoring the complicity of its own armed forces in widespread rape, the government is squarely at odds with donor countries such as the United States and Canada (whose companies have more than $3 billion in assets in the Congo). In 2010, Kabila's government grew tired of trying to appease western governments and signed a $6 billion trade and investment deal with China in exchange for infrastructure development. China did not concern itself with the lawlessness, lax human rights standards, and sordid abuses that define the Congo's mining sector. In keeping with its policy of non-state interference, China asked few questions and expected no answers.

Using mineral resources to fund conflict is not a new idea, of course. "Blood diamonds" played a key role in wars in Angola, Sierra Leone, and Liberia throughout the 1990s and beyond. But since 2003, the Kimberley Process has gone a long way towards eroding this practice. Under this scheme, the provenance of diamonds is certified to ensure that they do not come from sources tied to conflicts.* But no such process exists for coltan and other conflict minerals. Consumers cannot reliably know whether the components in their iPhones or video game systems contain ores from the Congo, Brazil, or Australia. The only appreciable difference is in the cost to manufacturers. Labour laws and human rights standards are expensive. While competition for the Congo's mining rights grows, some Australian mines are closing because they cannot compete with the Congo's "rollback pricing." The yearly tantalum market alone is now worth over $6 billion, half of which is used in the annual manufacturing of one billion cell phones. Electronics manufacturers can keep their profit margins high by using only the lowest-cost suppliers. In recent years, Sony, Apple, Hewlett-Packard, Sharp, Lenovo, IBM, Panasonic, Nintendo, Toshiba, and Samsung have been accused of failing to ensure that their supply chain doesn't lead back to conflict areas.

At a speech I gave in Waterloo, Ontario, a freshman engineering student asked why a Kimberley-type process couldn't be created for coltan and other minerals and metals used to fund conflicts. I liked the way he described it, as a "behavioural incentive." I began with the regrettable, "It's complicated." Then I

---

* In 2010, the Kimberley Process struggled to retain its relevance as Zimbabwe emerged as one of the largest diamond-producing countries in the world. With backing from India and China, the rapacious Robert Mugabe balked at international efforts to restrict the sale of Zimbabwe's diamonds, the mining of which led to forced labour and the deaths of about two hundred people.

spouted off the kind of elastic excuses worthy of a corporate public relations strategy: "There will never be consensus on the appropriate course of action"; "It's impossible to trace"; "An outright ban limits the opportunities to reform the sector from within"; "The revenues generated from resource extraction are necessary for reconstruction, if properly managed"; "What's needed is greater political will from African leaders themselves," and so on. He nodded politely and walked away.

It's not that these statements were untrue; it's just that these were obstacles, not answers. A few months later, a Canadian Member of Parliament, John McKay, introduced Bill C-300, a private member's bill that would have forced Canadian mining, oil, and gas companies to meet strict environmental and human rights standards when operating abroad. Companies failing to follow these guidelines would be denied government support. Over half of the world's exploration and mining companies are headquartered in Canada, and according to a never-released report commissioned by the Prospectors and Developers Association of Canada in 2009, Canadian mining companies with global explorations are involved in more than four times as many violations as the next two greatest offenders, Australia and India. Canada's mining sector aggressively lobbied against Bill C-300 and it was narrowly defeated 140 to 134. A friend who worked for a mining company with operations in several developing countries explained the bill's demise to me: "There's no way that legislation could have passed without some of Canada's biggest mining firms packing up and moving their headquarters elsewhere to avoid the hassle."

"Or," I shot back, "they could just do the right thing."

He looked at me with piteous amusement, and I felt a sudden solidarity with that engineering student in Waterloo. Still, there are lessons to be learned from the Kimberley Process when it comes to conflict minerals, including supply chain tracing, public pressure on manufacturers and retailers, political support for mining sector reform, and demilitarization of the industry within the Congo itself. But the challenges facing eastern Congo also highlight another weakness in international trade and development policy: unfettered economic investment and trade liberalization in unstable environments are locking impoverished but resource-rich countries in a perpetual state of violence.

Over the past decade, free market capitalism has been heralded as the next panacea of peace and prosperity for nations at the less-fortunate end of the Human Development Index.* The basic logic is that business creates jobs, which in turn foster wealth, promote stability, reduce aid dependency, and nurture a tax base that will finance social programs, including education and health, leading to more jobs, more stability, and so on. Jeffery Sachs, the Harvard economics professor and author of *Out of Poverty*, and Dambisa Moyo, Sachs's former pupil and author of *Dead Aid*, have both trumpeted the benefits of private sector investment in solving Africa's woes. Moyo, with an unassailable faith in "Foreign Direct Investment" (FDI), is even willing to overlook China's proclivity for shipping arms to many of Africa's despotic regimes. At a 2010 G20 meeting of finance ministers in Busan, South Korea, world leaders proposed a "new way forward" for countries in poverty. Guided by the experiences of Brazil, India, and South Korea, which promoted business development over aid, the ministers agreed to shift more donor funding to private-sector projects, increasing the budgets of the World

---

* The HDI is a yearly ranking that measures a country's social, economic, and political development.

Bank and the African Development Bank. All of this sounded eerily reminiscent of the failed "structural readjustment programs" of the 1980s. It's interesting that free market and capital cure-alls began to earn legitimacy as models for African prosperity at almost precisely the moment western economies, based on the same economic ideologies, took a sinus-piercing nose-dive. In unstable environments, the same variables that drove the collapse of Wall Street and led to the global financial meltdown of 2008 – namely, greed and weak regulatory mechanisms – are amplified. The only difference is that the profiteers wear fatigues instead of Armani suits, and trade Kalashnikovs, not credit default swaps.

This spectre of the "buy low, sell high" market economy lingers over Africa's most troubled regions, from the toxic sludge of the Niger Delta, to the charred villages of rural Darfur, to the amputee wards of Sierra Leone. Rather than solving Africa's challenges, unbridled capitalism threatens to make them exponentially worse, as countries with few natural resources of their own lay claim to the continent's vast agricultural land, oil reserves, minerals, metals, and timber. Resources are being bought and sold at an accelerated pace, and with a casual disregard for civilian welfare. There needs to be a critical review of governmental and private-sector practices when it comes to the plundering of Africa's wealth, and there must be stronger policy measures – nationally and internationally – to hold accountable those implicated in any transgressions. Armed conflict has persisted in the Congo not because of a lack of economic enterprise or financial capital. It has continued because these have not been accompanied by an equal investment in education and training (which would keep Congolese youth out of the militias and off the streets), disarmament, corporate social responsibility, peace-keeping, aid, law and order, and traditional diplomacy.

The Nadines of this world demonstrate this chronic imbalance between economic and development interests. Even if she sought justice, from whom would she seek it? After more than a decade of conflict, the country's legal infrastructure has been all but erased. A generation of the Congo's educated elite, including judges, teachers, lawyers, and assorted university graduates, were either systematically killed or fled the onslaught. Cases of rape in the Congo are rarely pursued because there is simply no one to prosecute them, to reach a verdict, or to carry out sentencing. The International Criminal Court has issued indictments against four of the Congo's war criminals who once incited thousands of young men, such as Nadine's rapists, to such sexual predation. But many others now retain senior posts in the Congolese army and are tasked with "protecting" civilians and mining areas. The thousands of Congolese women who have endured such atrocities could file a class-action lawsuit against the electronics industry, which puts the spoils of rape and war into the hands of consumers. But no precedent for such a lawsuit exists, and manufacturers can always hide behind the question of the minerals' origin. It may be worth pursuing, if only for the brief feeling of empowerment it might lend those who deserve to see a better day. But without stronger efforts to improve governance and address the corruption that exists across the Congo, any effort on a woman's part to seek justice will likely prove futile, if not risky. A woman I met in a displaced people's camp in Goma, eastern Congo, was sent to prison for two years because her husband paid a local politician $40 to "teach her a lesson" after she protested his decision to take a second wife.

At the same time, a consumer boycott of mobile phones and other products that may contain mementoes of the Congo's war is both impractical and unwarranted. Isolating Congo's mining sector only leads to more smuggling, and other opportunists simply fill the void. And closing the mines altogether, as the Congolese government has done on occasion in response to international pressure, unduly penalizes artisanal miners, exacerbating already disastrous levels of poverty throughout the region. The Enough Project makes several recommendations aimed at abolishing the illicit minerals trade. These include verifiable supply chains, infrastructure development that would provide employment opportunities to demobilized combatants (luring them away from mining areas and criminal gangs), and alternative livelihoods initiatives. In Sierra Leone, for example, aid and business groups including USAID, Tiffany jewellers, and the Foundation for Environmental Security and Sustainability launched a public-private partnership and have been successful at transforming land eroded by diamond mining into productive community and agricultural areas, raising standards of living and increasing local food production.

Other initiatives come at the problem from the other direction, putting the onus on the mining industry. Since 2002, the Publish What You Pay campaign has been overseen by a coalition of NGOs and civil society groups. The campaign calls on energy and mining companies to openly disclose their payments to governments in an effort to create greater transparency.

When the U.S. Congress passed the Dodd–Frank Wall Street Reform and Consumer Protection Act in July 2010, it included measures to ensure that "blood minerals" are not used in electronic devices. Although the law doesn't ban mineral imports, it does require U.S. manufacturers to demonstrate that their sourcing practices do not contribute to human rights abuses. Dodd-Frank has been fraught with difficulties at the implementation level, as local armed groups have found easy workarounds through Uganda and Rwanda. Furthermore, rather than wrestle with the complexities of adhering to Dodd-Frank, many American mining firms in eastern Congo simply shuttered their doors. Other initiatives include the creation of the Conflict-Free Smelter Program by the Washington-based Electronic Industry Citizenship Coalition, now the Responsible Business Alliance and the Brussels-based Global e-Sustainability Initiative. These industry groups aim to ensure that the coltan and other resources used by manufacturers does not originate from sources contributing to conflict in the DRC and elsewhere. But without mechanisms of enforceability, such initiatives are unlikely to change corporate behaviour in impoverished parts of the world. What's needed are serious financial penalties for compliance failures (which would be reinvested back into communities in the form of spending on health, educational, and social programs) and the threat of jail time for executives whose businesses can be linked to systemic abuses beyond our borders. This accountability gap could also be addressed in the years ahead by revising the ICC statute to include the jurisdiction to prosecute corporations whose activities can be linked to war crimes and crimes against humanity.

As Google demonstrated by flexing its muscle at China in response to their hacking into the Gmail accounts of human rights activists, technology companies have the power to stand on principle. If they are prepared to champion an international process with real teeth, then at least a "behavioural incentive" might begin to emerge. But it's naive to expect that voluntary industry initiatives alone will solve the problem. Just as with the Kimberley Process, success will hinge on the extent to which all the stakeholders, corporate, governmental, and non-governmental, are willing to mount a coordinated response and finance alternatives.

Without concerted, transformational change and a substantive investment in addressing the problems that plague eastern

Congo – from a feckless resource industry, to insipid corruption, to opportunistic governments, to a lacklustre United Nations peacekeeping effort, to the preponderance of small arms and chronically underfunded development programs – only one thing is certain: Nadine, and thousands like her, will certainly be raped again.

The director of the transit centre for newly demobilized youth, Michel, was in no mood to play host.

"If you want to speak to the boys, they're in there." He thrust his jaw towards a cinder-block warehouse surrounded by a nearly-four-metre perimeter wall capped with barbed wire. "We've worked with many international partners," he bemoaned. "They change every year. Leave any pens and writing books you have behind. We ran out three months ago."

At any given time, there were fifty to a hundred boys at the transit centre. Surrendered by their commanders as part of the peace negotiations, they were assembled in the bush and transported by MONUC (the UN mission in the Congo) to one of a few such centres in Bukavu, where they underwent basic counselling and schooling while the staff tried to trace whatever family might still be alive and willing to receive them. The bulletin boards of the onsite "family reunification" office had pictures of the boys with lists of names and locations, many crossed out. The average length of stay was three months, though children who proved harder to place could be there for twice as long. If no family members could be found, or if they refused the child's return (usually out of fear for their own safety, or because the community was likely to exact some form of vigilante justice), the child was much more likely to rejoin the militias immediately after being discharged. It was common practice for the same children to be handed over several times in the span of a few years, especially during the rainy season when it became more expensive to feed them.

Some of the boys lined up to greet me. "I was a porter," "I was a cook," "I was a lookout," they offered when introduced at the urging of an older boy, himself a "*chef d'équipe*," which I understood to mean that he had participated in direct combat. I've met dozens of child soldiers over the past fifteen years – in Liberia, Uganda, Sierra Leone, Somalia, Burundi, and the Congo. I've noted how consistently they self-identify as either leaders or subordinates, even several years later. Even though many who claim only to have carried food or tended fires are usually lying about their involvement in atrocities, they are at least empathetic enough to be embarrassed by it. Most worrisome are the young sociopaths who, with a fatuous grin, spout off the number of people they killed, the villages they torched, and the limbs they cut off. They have fetishized their crimes, and will even exaggerate the morbid details for the pleasure of provoking fear and disgust. The rate of recidivism among this latter group is high, and those who don't end up back with the militias typically form gangs who go on raping, smuggling, and stealing.

Inside, the warehouse was a barracks-style dorm where children were divided according to age and slept two to a cot, or on a plastic mat on the floor. There was a stench of urine in the corridors. If there were any windows, I failed to notice them. In the first room, younger children flicked cards at a bottle cap, while a boy who looked to be twelve years old openly masturbated a few feet from them. He smiled at me when I walked in, then put more effort into the task. The other boys laughed. "Well, at least one of you has a job," I joked, intent on proving that it would take far more than that to rile me.

After spending several hours evaluating the services offered by the centre, I walked with Michel to my vehicle. "Did you get the information you needed to form an opinion?" he asked, in his perfunctory style. I had: the lamentable irony of most DDR programs is that only the second "D" (demobilization) actually holds for any length of time. With so little investment in reintegration and rehabilitation, the first "D" (disarmament) is rarely realized. The centre wasn't failing these boys; everything outside of it was.

In the immediate aftermath of the war in early 2000, Sierra Leone had better-funded, more-comprehensive DDR programs than any I have since witnessed in the Congo. During visits I made to similar transit centres in Freetown, ex-combatants tearfully spoke of the pain of their rehabilitation process, and of being haunted by the final dignity of their victims as they slit their throats or sawed through their wrists. These former child soldiers were resolute in their conviction that they would never return to the life that now tormented them. One month later, during an uprising in Freetown, Foday Sankoh, founder and leader of Sierra Leone's Revolutionary United Front (RUF), visited several of the centres I'd just returned from. I learned that the same boys who'd spoken so eloquently of the shame and abuse they'd suffered as RUF soldiers quickly fell into formation and pleaded with him to be redeployed.

Deeply traumatized, the boys are estranged from the emotional cues that guide social behaviour. They struggle to delineate right from wrong, pleasure from violence, and affection from control. Those who have been rehabilitated, such as Ishmael Beah (author of the book *A Long Way Gone*, about his experiences as a child soldier in Sierra Leone) and Emmanuel Jal (a hip-hop artist, spokesperson for Amnesty International and Oxfam, and one of Sudan's "Lost Boys"), have described their difficult rehabilitation processes. These former child soldiers received considerably more support than most, and completed their recovery in the United States and the United Kingdom, respectively, far removed from the ongoing violence that the vast majority of demobilized child soldiers return to.

As I climbed into the vehicle, Michel left me to find a security guard to open the gate. A young boy, not one I'd been introduced to, rapped at my window. He pressed his thumb to his index finger and brought it up to his mouth. He wanted food.

"I'm sorry," I explained, lowering my window, "I don't have any. And it wouldn't be fair to the other boys."

The boy's expression changed: my response had enraged him. "*Argent! Argent!*" he shouted: Money! Money!

"*Faites attention!*" my driver hissed, as six other boys came running from the dorm. Mayi-Mayi soldiers had once attacked his village and, he'd declared during the drive over, as far as he was concerned all of these boys were criminals and did not warrant the sympathy of foreigners. A few stood at the front, pounding on the hood, while two others mounted the back bumper and one jumped on the roof. They forcefully rocked the car back and forth, screaming at us to hand over everything we had, while the boy outside my window squealed with delight. My driver pounded heavily on the horn and, shaking his head, released the clutch. The car lurched forward abruptly. Now they were even angrier. They kicked the doors as he tried, as best he could, to inch forward without hurting them. I looked behind to see Michel running towards us, flailing his arms, commanding the boys to stop. As the security guard opened the gate, the boy at my window leaned in and said, "The next time you come here without any money, we're going to rape you, pour gasoline on you, and set you on fire."

CHAPTER 3

WINNING WARS, LOSING PEACE

There are known knowns. These are things we know that we know.
There are known unknowns. That is to say, there are things that we
now know we don't know. But there are also unknown unknowns.
There are things we do not know we don't know.
DONALD RUMSFELD, FEBRUARY 2002

On March 20, 2003, wave after wave of Tomahawk cruise missiles ripped through Baghdad's ancient streets, crumbling minarets, Tree of Life mosaics, and Ottoman archways, hitting markets, homes, and palaces, and paralyzing the ministries of Foreign Affairs and Planning, as well as Iraq's national TV station and its major telecommunications centre. The "Shock and Awe" campaign was executed with such cadence and pyrotechnic force that the only thing missing was a soundtrack. In the first twenty-four hours alone, 1,500 bombs and missiles fell on Baghdad. By the end of the initial invasion phase, some 7,500 Iraqis had died and almost 18,000 were injured. That was the "shock."

The "awe" was that the Ministry of Oil was left untouched and swiftly protected after U.S. Marines claimed Baghdad on April 4. In short order, Iraq's history, from Sumerian artifacts, to birth and employment records, to weapons caches and Saddam's ill-gotten wealth, were pillaged by a newly "liberated" people.

It was clear, even in those early days, that the United States and its allies had technically won the war but were about to experience a local public relations defeat from which they would never recover. I've spent considerable time in Iraq since the mid 1990s and have travelled to the country multiple times over a span of nearly a decade. But returning to Baghdad within days of the toppling of Saddam's regime, I was struck by how disconnected America's military leadership was from the Iraqi psyche. While all but the staunchest Ba'athists were happy to see the back end of Saddam, Iraqis were also deeply suspicious of American intentions. Saddam had spent years manipulating an isolated people into believing that the enemy without (America and its western allies) was far more threatening than his own murderous regime. During my many conversations with Iraqis since the 1991 Gulf War, I noted a shift in the public mood. Iraqi youth, in particular, gradually abandoned their victimhood ("Can the world not see our suffering?") in favour of a kind of resilient militancy that was unsettling ("We must fight the western imperial aggressors who want our oil!"). It left me with an abiding sense, even before this latest war, that the country was destined for calamity. In the weeks following the arrival of U.S. forces in Baghdad, the lawlessness, the slow progress in rebuilding Iraq's shattered infrastructure, the collapse of the country's public service which employed 40 percent of the population, and the appropriation of Saddam's palaces all served to compound Iraqi bitterness.

With Saddam out of the way, extremists of all persuasions harnessed this resentment to cultivate a legion of suicide bombers and other foot soldiers whose anger was easily co-opted by fundamentalist, ethnocentric ideology. This was the great American miscalculation in Iraq. Through sheer strategic incompetence, the 2003 war rendered unto Al-Qaeda what

Al-Qaeda had, until that point, been unable to render unto itself.

The pristine condition of the Ministry of Oil became something of a scandal. "Is this not proof of American intentions in invading Iraq?" was an accusation I heard from cabbies, fixers, doctors, academics, and even a few journalists and international aid workers. If it's possible for one trait to define a population, in Iraq it was pride – and that pride was offended by what transpired on the ground during those few short weeks after George W. Bush declared "Mission Accomplished" on May 1.

The response to U.S. and Coalition troops in Iraq varied across the country, but Baghdad is Iraq's cultural, political, and historic centre. The city is situated on the Tigris River in the Fertile Crescent, whose ancient Mesopotamian civilizations yielded philosophy, the measurement of time, and the rule of law. Outside of the Kurdish areas, even moderate Iraqis felt the U.S. occupation of Baghdad bordered on the criminal. At the very least, most found it crude, distasteful, and disrespectful.

For the foreign visitor, there is a natural order to building relationships in Iraq: introductions, followed by tea served in gold-painted ornamental glasses and drinkable only with copious amounts of sugar,[*] leading to the affairs of the day and an empirical debate on whatever captures the host's interest. Prior to March 2003, this all occurred in the presence of government-appointed minders, who minded only if you strayed into criticizing "Baba Saddam." (In true fascist form, Iraqi children were taught to use this name, which means "father," and could

---

[*] During the economic sanctions, sugar became prohibitively expensive for most Iraqi families. As was the custom, this luxury item was therefore reserved for guests, especially foreign ones, who often failed to notice when they were alone in reaching for the teaspoon.

often be overheard singing about their leader in the playground. One dirge sung by schoolchildren translates to "Saddam, Saddam, we will give our blood for you.") While setting up humanitarian programs in Iraq, it was normal for me to get through no more than two meetings a day. To rush the process was considered crass and insensitive, despite how indulgent it felt to someone raised with a puritanical, high-velocity work ethic.

Military protocol in post-Saddam Iraq didn't just minimize these interactions with Iraqi civil society, it avoided them altogether. The U.S.-led forces established fortified enclaves and distributed lucrative contracts, which amounted to $18.4 billion in the first year alone, to American firms with strong Republican Party ties. These companies then lorded their "special privilege" over the millions of unemployed Iraqis and those whose life savings had been erased by more than a dozen years of crippling economic sanctions. Bush and Tony Blair could say whatever they wanted about "regime change" and the "liberation" of Iraq's people, but on the ground any goodwill that may have existed was squandered before the spin cycle even kicked in.

My first order of business in Iraq was to organize a shipment of humanitarian supplies to a pediatric hospital in Karbala whose doctors I'd known for many years. Baghdad had become a city I no longer recognized. It had been subsumed by foreign journalists, military personnel, aid workers, tanks, checkpoints, and vendors hawking American goods such as Duracell batteries, Dentyne gum, Doritos, and Crest toothpaste, which were technically still contraband as the sanctions had not yet been formally lifted.

U.S. Central Command announced there would be a briefing for aid agencies and journalists at the Palestine Hotel to review security conditions along the country's main roads. A number of organizations were there, represented by their senior staff, most of whom had absolutely no experience in Iraq and little familiarity with the context. This was hardly surprising, as few international aid agencies were granted entry into Iraq under Saddam, who never failed to recognize the propaganda value of a dying child.

Seated beside me during the briefing was my friend and colleague Margaret Hassan. At fifty-eight years old, Margaret was a British national married to an Iraqi, and had lived in Iraq for thirty years. She had endured Saddam Hussein, the 1991 Gulf War, and more than a decade of economic sanctions. Since 1991, she'd been coping with Iraq's malnourished, sick, and unaccompanied children as director of CARE International in Iraq. To many aid community veterans she was a hero (though she would have bristled at the suggestion) because she'd persevered, even as the rest recoiled. Margaret was, as *The Guardian* once described her, "articulate and forthright," and a relentless critic of United Nations sanctions in Iraq.

On this occasion, Margaret's mood alternated between exasperation and indignation. She would shake her head or exhale emphatically whenever she found cause for disagreement, which was often. I found it hard not to encourage her public disapprovals, in part for the sheer entertainment value – Margaret could simultaneously alienate the military and the aid community with one derisive comment – but mostly because she was usually *right*.

Colonel King, a U.S. Forces representative for humanitarian affairs, invoked ire during his welcoming remarks by parroting "we're liberators, not occupiers." A middle-aged Iraqi doctor was the first to respond, which he did with exhausted composure. "I will tell you something very important," he said directly to King. "Whenever Saddam came into our streets, people would cheer. In the same way, when Americans come into our streets, people cheer. But just like we did with Saddam, when you walk away, we say 'motherfuckers.'"

King seemed genuinely hurt by this. Convinced of America's moral legitimacy in overthrowing Saddam and his vile sycophants, it was my impression that King and other senior officers in attendance were struggling to comprehend what they were hearing from aid workers and Iraqi citizens. After all, Iraqi children *were* applauding American tanks on Baghdad streets. But the military was alienated from the Iraqi experience; they couldn't understand how adept people had become at giving, as Orwell wrote, "the appearance of solidity to pure wind." (Orwell was speaking of political language, but the description can be fairly applied to Iraqis as well, who were required to wave flags in its gale.)

With all the media in the room, and multiple NGOs competing for their attention, it didn't take long for the grandstanding to begin. A newly arrived senior representative from Save the Children U.S. rose to his feet to deliver a heartfelt soliloquy on the sorry state of Iraq's children, urging America to "do something." He rhymed off a list of dreary statistics about how mortality rates and malnutrition had increased dramatically during the previous decade. This was too much for Margaret to bear. "With all due respect," she shot back from across the room, "child malnutrition is a chronic problem in this country. The sanctions made it exponentially worse, but that didn't seem to matter back then. The government developed a complex system for delivering monthly food rations to impoverished families. Those supplies are about to run out, and all those records are presently being set alight or discarded. The people who used to manage the program have all been let go and no one has any way of knowing who they were. *That's* now the problem. So please, don't waste any more of our time telling us things we already know." Then, leaning into me, she muttered, "I've had just about enough of this nonsense."

"Margaret," I cautioned, "this is only the beginning."

Not long afterwards, Margaret and I shared a ride to the Green Zone at the invitation of Colonel King. U.S. commanders wanted to be kept apprised of the humanitarian priorities and to discuss "NGO coordination." That the military believed such coordination was possible spoke to the massive ideological divide between the two sectors.

"This is ridiculous. Just leave us here," Margaret said, directing her driver to drop us at a military checkpoint near the entrance to the Republican Palace. "This traffic is unbearable." The trip, which normally took ten minutes, had lasted more than two hours. "They just put these barricades up wherever they want. It is shutting the city down. We can't live like this."

During the drive, I was surprised by how many of Saddam's portraits had yet to be defaced: Saddam firing a Kalashnikov, Saddam saluting the masses, Saddam posing as a fighter pilot, Saddam carrying children on his shoulders. The public euphoria of felling his bronzed statue in Firdos Square appeared to have been quickly replaced with a kind of nervous hesitancy. Without proof of Saddam's death or capture, it was clear he would continue to cast a pall over Iraqi lives. Such was the awful paradox of the Iraqi condition at the "end" of the war (and before its conspicuous evolution to a far more lethal, anti-civilian variety): Iraqis' antipathy towards the future made it virtually impossible to move beyond the paranoia of the past.

Margaret grabbed her notebook and a pen from the dash and pointed to an address. "We need to go here!" she insisted, ripping the page from the book and handing it to a young

Marine (they are always younger than I imagine them to be) at the palace entrance.

"Yes, ma'am," he responded with polite deference. "I understand. But you must all go through the inspection, and then a bus will pick you up on the other side and take you to your destination. Now you need to tell your driver to move his car. This area is off limits."

Beyond the concrete barriers and sandbags that served as a perimeter, soldiers checked our passports, emptied our bags, and patted us down. Passing through the snare of Humvees, machine guns, and human congestion and into the palace courtyard, with its manicured rose gardens and lush embankments, I felt as if we'd just fallen down Alice's rabbit hole. In front of us lay a world of cleanliness, order, and efficiency. Behind us was a world where grief-stricken families scavenged lists taped to emergency room walls for identifying details among the charred and fragmented bodies piled in hospitals and morgues. Ambulance sirens screamed in the distance, but never approached. Like everything else in the city, they were stalled behind checkpoints, closed streets, and suffocating traffic. Not that they could provide much service anyway; Iraq's hospitals were desperately short of supplies. It wasn't unusual for staff to remove gauze bandages from lacerated limbs, then rinse and reapply them to new arrivals. Electricity was available only sporadically, and then for only a few hours at a time – enough power for a handful of guests in Saddam's preferred hotels to shower, but not enough to pump the city's sewage, which backed up into the streets.

Electricity was a constant challenge in Iraq. The power grid had been deliberately destroyed by Coalition Forces during the first Gulf War. Crippling economic sanctions, compounded by bureaucratic incompetence, complex United Nations approval processes, Saddam's ongoing antagonisms, and corruption within the Oil for Food Programme, further prevented Iraqis from rebuilding their electrical infrastructure, which functioned at a fraction of its pre-1991 levels. What military ends were served in "smart" bombing Iraq back to a pre-industrial age remained to be seen, but the civilian impact was swift and cataclysmic: outbreaks of diarrheal diseases, measles, typhoid, and other epidemics began within days of severing the power supply. Sewage could no longer be pumped or treated; medications, vaccines, and blood products requiring refrigeration spoiled, and water sources quickly became contaminated. By the end of the 1990s, UNICEF was reporting that war and sanctions had caused hundreds of thousands of deaths among Iraqi children under five.

Yet in the aftermath of the first Gulf War, this unfolding civilian tragedy was mostly met with indifference and callousness by western policymakers such as Madeleine Albright, the U.S. ambassador to the United Nations (and later secretary of state to Bill Clinton). When asked about the ballooning death rate among Iraqi children during an interview with Leslie Stahl on *60 Minutes* in 1996, Albright was unflinching. "I think this is a very hard choice, but the price – we think the price is worth it." For more than a decade, each side blamed the other for killing Iraq's children. While Saddam availed himself of every last shroud to invoke sympathy within Iraq and the rest of the Arab world, political pundits asserted on CNN and *Meet the Press* that the power to end Iraqi suffering rested uniquely with their barbarous dictator, who needed only to comply with UN demands. That all parties to the conflict would engage in this kind of asymmetrical warfare in which civilians, though not the target *ab initio*, were so irrefutably dying is further proof of the moral relativism that perverts political thinking during war.

Sixty years after the Geneva Conventions, civilians make up a larger proportion of deaths in war than at any other time in modern history. During World War I, 15 percent of those who died were civilians. In World War II, it was about half. For the past two decades, 80 percent of those dying in wars have been civilians.* Instead of reducing civilian casualties, advanced weapons systems have had the opposite effect – an outcome Iraqis were painfully familiar with.

———

INSIDE THE PALACE, Margaret and I sat at the end of a grand mahogany table alongside other aid workers. Everything about the situation was emblematic of the moral qualms international humanitarian organizations face while fulfilling their mandate. There we were, inside one of Saddam's wretched extravagances, unsure whether we should express outrage over the military's handling of civilian affairs or outline a strategy to meet the most pressing relief needs. A few agencies had refused to attend the meeting, arguing that it would interfere with their neutrality and independence. But most saw no alternative: the U.S. Forces in Baghdad were the de facto governing body at the time. There wasn't even a way for aid workers to legally obtain a visa to enter the country and formally establish their operations. Relief shipments were being held up at the borders because no one knew

---

* There is academic disagreement about the accuracy of these statistics and the validity of comparing wars in different eras, since reporting practices have changed. For an epidemiological argument to be sound, apples should always be compared to apples, which is difficult when analyzing mortality data spanning 100 years. Unfortunately, the lack of robust reporting on the civilian impact of war is not only a major obstacle in policy debate, but also creates room for deniability among those who wage war.

what signatures were required, or who was authorized to make such approvals. Humanitarian organizations had little choice but to negotiate with the U.S. command in Iraq. Aid workers could either risk being perceived as militarily aligned and become the soft target of escalating anti-western sentiment, or pack up and go home, knowing that people would die as a result. Given that civilians were already dying at alarming rates, and that it would take years for Iraq's health and social infrastructures to be rebuilt, those on the ground searched for ways to make peace with their principles.

A stocky, pugilistic general, whose name I missed, positioned himself at the head of the table while officers in the room stood to attention. The invited guests – in sneakers, khakis, and fraying scarves – ignored protocol and didn't rise.

"You are convened here this afternoon," the general began, "so that we might gain your valuable insights into the psychology and needs of the Iraqi people at this difficult time. What do you want us to know?"

Curiously, apart from Margaret, not a single Iraqi citizen was present to answer the question. As soon as the silence became tedious, a few people offered their observations.

"The banks urgently need to reopen."

"The monthly food rations must be reinstituted until an alternative solution can be found."

"Instruct your border troops to issue blanket approvals for all vaccines and essential medicines."

"I appreciate the time you've taken today," interjected the general in a manner that was more bored than rude. "Let's continue to work together. Good luck with your efforts."

Suddenly Margaret, who had been uncharacteristically silent, leaned forward, pressing her forearms into the table. "So that's it, then? You asked us here to tell you how the Iraqi people are feeling?" Her voice was fierce. "Can you not see it for yourselves? You have invaded their country. You control their movements. You have taken over Saddam's palaces. You smoke his cigars and swim in his pools. You have armed guards in front of a pristine Ministry of Oil while the Ministry of Health is looted and burned. Their children cannot go to school because there are unexploded bombs in the playgrounds. Their loved ones die while ambulances are delayed at checkpoints. Family and friends are detained without explanation, and imprisoned in the same torture cells that Saddam used. And you want to know what they think about all of this?" She paused to collect herself. "I will tell you. The truth is they do not see a difference between you and *him*."

The general acknowledged her comments then walked out, as a junior officer thanked us for our participation.

We left the palace and Margaret radioed her driver to collect us. She was calmer than I'd seen her in years – not self-satisfied, but hopeful that she may have been heard.

"I admire your courage, Margaret," I said later in the car, as we pulled over a short distance from the checkpoint in front of my hotel.

"It's not courage," she joked. "I've just been at this so long that I don't know when to shut up. Watch, now I'll end up on a no-fly list."

"I wouldn't be surprised," I said. "Listen, I may not see you for a while. I'm off to Karbala tomorrow."

"The roads should be safe. I've not heard of any recent issues. I'll give you a ring if anything useful comes out of one of these meetings."

"That assumes you'll still be invited."

She laughed and waved goodbye as I got out. As the car turned around, I could hear her driver, through his open window, peppering Margaret with questions about what she'd seen inside Saddam's palace. He had paid a tremendous price for his dictator's outrageous comforts, and he wanted to know precisely how many Hussein family portraits and Persian carpets his dead relatives had been worth.

At the checkpoint, a nineteen-year-old Marine stopped me and asked, with a Midwestern lilt, "Where'd y'all come from?"

I thought he wanted to know my nationality. "Canada."

"No," he said, sounding exasperated. "I mean, how'd you get *here*?"

I said I'd driven from Jordan, posing as a journalist.

"Oh," he replied, kicking his boots against the curb to clear them of dust, a futile exercise in Baghdad if ever there was one. "I'm not sure where that is. We just arrived in tanks two days ago. I don't really have a sense of where I am. I mean, I know I'm in Baghdad, but other than that . . . I guess I should have asked more questions." He seemed genuinely interested and well-meaning.

I felt for this young man, who seemed as unsure about his reasons for waging war as he was of the geography. At one point he asked me whether I'd been to Iraq before, and if people understood they were now "free." This was not a question that could be answered in absolutes, at the side of a road, while visibly irked civilians surrendered their personal effects for inspection. I said only that the Iraqis I knew were glad to put the tyranny of Saddam Hussein behind them. He told me he looked forward to the day when he could bring his future children to Iraq on vacation and show them what he'd been a part of. He wanted to know whether I believed that would one day be possible. It was hard not to admire his earnestness, especially after having met his supervisors.

As he completed a routine search of my bag, he found my business card and asked, "What kind of doctor are you?"

"A medical doctor. For women and children mostly."

"Can you wait here? We could use your help with something." He ran toward a slight young woman, the first female Marine I'd seen in Baghdad, and handed her my card. I expected her to have some kind of medical problem that she was too embarrassed to disclose to her base doctors. Instead, she walked to a grassy area overlooking the Tigris and returned carrying a toddler.

"Can you help him?" she asked anxiously. "He's been here for a few days with his sister, who isn't much older. I've offered them food, but he won't eat."

I reached into my bag for my stethoscope, which I often carry with me in the field for moments like these. His heartbeat was shallow, languid. His chest crackled. Pneumonia, malnutrition, dehydration. He was dying: from war, and sanctions, and chronic poverty.

"I'll arrange for him to be transported to the pediatric hospital," I offered. "I know some of the doctors there and they'll do everything they can. He's very lucky to have found you."

IN KARBALA, the doctors I'd known for many years before the war were both excited and stunned to see me pull up to the pediatric hospital. They were overjoyed because I was laden with supplies: medications, bandages, IV bags, sutures, and other materials I had been able to procure in neighbouring Jordan. I had a good sense of their needs, having visited the hospital a month before the war and been provided with a list of urgent requests. But they had not expected to see me arrive in a vehicle with "TV" in duct tape on everything but the windshield. In other war zones I'd worked in, it was the journalists who pretended to be aid workers to gain access.

Karbala is one of the holiest cities for Shia Muslims. It is the site of the tomb of Husayn ibn Ali, the Prophet Muhammad's grandson. The Muslim caliph was beheaded in Karbala in 680 CE. My visit coincided with the start of the annual pilgrimage (second only to Mecca for Shia Muslims) to the gloriously mirrored Imam Husayn Shrine,* during which hundreds of thousands arrive from all over the Arab world. To the outside observer, the pilgrimage is a disconcerting mix of ritual adulation, shrill threnodies, and macabre flagellation that stretches for kilometres along the highways into Karbala. Women in black niqabs wail and carry their children, as men beat themselves with chains and swords. I knew from the security briefings that U.S. Central Command was concerned that the pilgrimage might devolve into anti-American protests and attacks against their troops, who were positioned all along the route in tanks and armoured personnel carriers. They also suspected pro-Saddam forces were preparing an assault on the parading Shias.

In 1991, American forces had recognized Iraq's internal religious tensions as an opportunity. Shia Muslims generally disliked Saddam, who had both offended and subjugated them. During the height of the war, President George H. W. Bush broadcast a

---

* I'd once been granted special permission to enter this shrine, even though non-Muslims (especially women) are prohibited. The offer came after an absurd meeting during which I'd been interviewing the mosque's clerics for an international sanctions report. Although I was respectfully covered, the clerics could not address me directly, as a non-observant woman. So whenever I asked a question, they would animatedly answer the only empty chair in the room. This went on for hours. I'm quite sure they offered me the tour only because I'd put up with the charade. The repeating squares of mirror and glass in the interior of the Shrine are truly an architectural wonder.

message and air-dropped pamphlets encouraging Shias to rise up. Heeding the call, Karbala became the site of the largest uprising against the Republican Guard. However, when the promised American support failed to materialize, the Republican Guard moved in with tanks, slaughtering tens of thousands of Shias. Even the pediatric hospital was overtaken by Saddam's troops. During my first visit to Iraq in the mid 1990s, staff doctors took me into several unoccupied rooms that had been used as torture chambers to bludgeon or electrocute suspected dissidents. Blood stains were still visible on the concrete floors beneath corroding metal cots. For Saddam, it wasn't enough to mutilate and then kill his opponents: he *obliterated* them, which he accomplished with efficiency by issuing orders to execute entire families. One of the resident doctors, Dr. Ali, had been held by the Republican Guard and ordered to provide medical assistance to their injured ranks. "At night," he told me, in a diesel-soaked hallway* as he was finishing his rounds, "when I close my eyes, I must first wait for the screams in my mind to stop."

In the decade that followed the Shia uprising, Saddam systematically discriminated against Karbala's civilian population. Even as sanctions policy began to make exemptions on humanitarian grounds, Karbala's residents continued to experience massive shortages in food, medicines, and salaries for public-sector workers. Dr. Ali slept on a urine-stained mattress every night on the mortar-ruined top floor of the hospital and earned $20 a

---

* As with everything else under the sanctions, cleaning agents (including hospital disinfectants) could not be imported. Hospitals would routinely mix diesel fuel with water and use it to wash floors, mattresses, and even operating tables. As someone who suffers from mild asthma, I would find it hard to breathe after a few minutes and need to step outside. I can only imagine how hard it was for people admitted to the wards with respiratory illnesses.

month. The Iraqi Red Crescent Society, administratively controlled by Ba'ath Party stooges until 2003, offered little by way of assistance. The gaps in medical and social services in Karbala were enormous by Iraqi standards even before the 2003 Iraq War, and I was under no illusion that the supplies our team had scraped together would last longer than a week.

As I was leaving, the hospital staff made the same desperate plea: when I return to Baghdad, I must talk about the gravity of the situation in Karbala and ask for medications, supplies, and money for salaries to be urgently sent. But who was going to listen? The window of confusion at the Jordanian border during the early days of U.S. command over Iraq, which made it possible for me to bring supplies into the country without paperwork, was rapidly closing. It was unclear how, or whether, I might be able to assist in the coming weeks. Even United Nations agencies were facing the same quandaries as the NGOs. When General Colin Powell's shoddy evidence of Iraq's Weapons of Mass Destruction scheme failed to move the UN Security Council, UN agencies became non-aligned actors in a U.S.-led war. It was my impression that UN organizations on the ground were being treated by U.S. commanding authorities with more derision than other aid groups. Bush's "you're either with us or against us" approach to diplomacy infiltrated all levels of decision making during the long aftermath of the war, penalizing Iraqi civilians most of all. And the military was providing little space for an independent humanitarian response: this was *their* war and everyone else had to play by their rules, which they were figuring out as they went along.

Not long after my visit to Karbala, the roads became too insecure to travel, and violence against aid agencies began to escalate. On August 19, 2003, a flatbed truck carrying explosives drove into the United Nations headquarters at the Canal Hotel in Baghdad, killing twenty-two people, including the UN's top envoy to Iraq, Sergio Vieira de Mello, and UNICEF Iraq's program coordinator, Christopher Klein-Beekman. It was a devastating attack unleashed against a civilian target amidst growing anti-western sentiment. Such failure to respect the rules of war on all sides – from the abhorrent treatment of prisoners at Abu Ghraib by American forces, to the brutalization of civilians by terrorist groups, to the military's engagement in aid operations for political ends – dealt a serious blow to the humanitarian community's capacity to help civilians in Iraq. It was the product of a disturbing trend that may be irreversible.

Over the past decade, the defence ministries of western nations have begun taking a more hands-on approach to humanitarian operations, particularly in countries such as Iraq and Afghanistan in which they are militarily engaged. In a sense, it is one step further along the "militarized humanitarian intervention force" continuum. Now western militaries are no longer charged only with securing areas, preventing further atrocities, and allowing for the safe and effective delivery of humanitarian aid. They also assume the role of delivering ever larger proportions of aid budgets, in the form of school and hospital reconstruction initiatives and other goodwill endeavours. In this anti-terrorism, counter-insurgency military environment, victory, to the extent that one is attainable, is tied to public opinion. Insofar as western militaries in Afghanistan and Iraq are striving to promote security by ending authoritarian rule, achieving democratic development, and advancing women's rights, success hinges on local acceptance. To win militarily, the advantages of such propositions must be heard and felt by communities.

This is not a new strategy. The phrase "winning hearts and minds" was coined by British military commander Sir Gerald Templer, Director of Operations and High Commissioner for Malaya. During the Malayan "Emergency" of the 1950s, he was tasked with restoring order (while protecting British investments) in the former colony, which he accomplished by appeasing civilians with health and social services. Tactically speaking, western militaries are better served, both domestically and internationally, by hard-selling their softer side. Aid is even described in a 2009 "Commanders' Guide to Money as a Weapons System" (an army manual for American troops in Iraq and Afghanistan) as a "non lethal weapon." And media coverage of NATO forces building schools and high-fiving the locals is, in terms of solidifying public support for the mission, an effective antidote to stories of western soldiers amputating trophy fingers from dead Taliban fighters or accidentally bombing wedding parties.

Placing humanitarian efforts under the aegis of the military is an increasingly risky strategy, one with devastating consequences for soldiers, civilians, and aid workers. And there is no actual evidence to suggest that the military is any more efficient, effective, or responsive when it comes to aid and development than traditional NGOs. On the contrary, they are far more expensive and markedly less successful at it. The militarization of aid also takes liberties with people's lives by politicizing that which ought not to be political.

Between 2002 and 2005, the proportion of U.S. aid money controlled by the Pentagon increased from 6 percent to 22 percent and now exceeds 35 percent. In Afghanistan alone, by the end of 2009, international military forces had delivered approximately $1.7 billion in aid and development, primarily through private contractors, military-dominated Provincial Reconstruction Teams

(PRTs), and the Commander's Emergency Response Program (CERP). U.S. Special Forces and Canadian troops have also been directly involved in a wide array of "hearts and minds" initiatives in Afghanistan. In addition to counter-insurgency efforts, the troops now repair and rebuild mosques, reconstruct schools and medical clinics, and distribute food and clothing. Photos and stories of their endeavours make for compelling Facebook entries and feature articles by embedded journalists. But they overshadow a far more significant debate about the appropriateness of such interventions and the security risks associated with them.

Unfortunately, there are many examples of how serious these risks are. PRT efforts in Afghanistan are popular targets of insurgents, with significantly higher casualty rates than exist among non-militarized NGO projects. There are PRTs in thirty-three out of thirty-four provinces in Afghanistan. These are heavily guarded initiatives that, in many instances, assume a development role traditionally undertaken by humanitarian organizations, such as building schools, providing clean drinking water, training, and improving access to health care. Canadian, German, American, and Swedish troops working on PRT projects have been killed, along with hundreds of civilian workers. By comparison, most aid agencies implement similar programs without armed guards and maintain a clear distinction from the International Security Assistance Forces. And PRT schools are seen by Afghans themselves to be far more vulnerable to targeting by insurgents or criminal gangs when compared to NGO-supported schools. Understandably, parents who worry that their children's school is at greater risk of attack will also be more inclined to keep them home, decreasing attendance rates.

The military asserts that NGOs do not have the capacity in war-torn environments to deliver large-scale projects in insecure areas, and that the frequency of attacks on PRTs is simply a product of geography, as military aid programs concentrate on front-line communities. But this too is a problematic strategy: military aid spending in Afghanistan has disproportionately focused on volatile provinces while other areas are overlooked, despite their potential to model the way. And the presumption that the military can spend aid dollars and demonstrate results more quickly and efficiently, given their logistical and technical advantages, than traditional aid and development organizations is false. Just over half of CERP funds allocated to the military between 2004 and 2009 for aid projects in Afghanistan were actually disbursed. In addition, CERP funding was frequently awarded to private contractors and local officials, with little or no administrative oversight, and has been subject to widespread allegations of corruption and profiteering. The military's emphasis has historically been on showing that the funds were spent, not on what happened once these funds were off the books. The U.S. Government Accountability Office has reported fraud and mismanagement related to military and private-sector reconstruction initiatives in Iraq and Afghanistan, in the order of tens of billions of dollars, distributed to American firms such as Halliburton, DynCorp International, and KBR (Kellogg, Brown, and Root). Money meant for development and reconstruction programs appears to have simply evaporated.

In addition to CERT- and PRT-related aid forays, the military has also taken on a more prominent role during humanitarian emergencies, with mixed results. In 2001, responding to threats of famine during the aerial bombardment of Afghanistan, the United States dropped 1.5 million daily ration packages, containing rice, vegetables, and fruit. These packages were the same size and colour as the cluster bombs also dropped in the vicinity at the time. Not surprisingly, some civilians lethally confused the two. Aerial food drops are of questionable effectiveness even under ideal conditions. In this case, the packages often broke upon impact, and many were collected and sold for profit by local warlords. British Forces in southern Iraq also ventured into similar relief distributions, off-loading bottled water to desperate Iraqis from the back of military trucks. These operations quickly degenerated into angry riots. There are tried-and-tested methods of conducting safe and efficient relief distributions. Tossing supplies from the back of a truck at an exasperated mob is not one of them.

Canada's DART (Disaster Assistance Response Team) program was created by the Canadian Forces in 1996 as a response to failed humanitarian efforts during Rwanda's cholera epidemic. DART is a military rapid-response team that arrives at disaster sites (upon invitation from the United Nations or the target country) as a means of bridging the gap until longer-term help arrives. It has been used in response to disasters in Honduras, Turkey, Sri Lanka, Pakistan, and Haiti, with mixed results. DART has been criticized, particularly by seasoned relief groups, for its late arrival on many missions and its high cost of deployment. As one example, the cost of DART's response to the 2004 Indian Ocean tsunami was estimated at $20 million and the operation was called "amateur." Former Canadian Prime Minister Paul Martin, writing in his memoirs *Hell or High Water: My Life In and Out of Politics*, wrote about DART's deployment to Indonesia, "The truth is that we probably could have provided clean water cheaply and more rapidly than DART was able to do. . . . It was important for Canadians to see tangible evidence of our commitment to the relief effort. It gave Canadians a human connection with the efforts of their country to help." While the concept of a "rapid response" team of experts, from doctors to engineers, is politically appealing, in most instances it has been too slow and expensive to be of practical benefit. DART's public relations value has trumped rational decision making.

Military efforts to respond to the 2010 Haiti earthquake suffered similar setbacks. The United States, which deployed 14,000 troops to Haiti and put its military in charge of the mission, was accused of favouring Americans and wealthy citizens over those in poorer, less safe neighbourhoods in its rescue operations. After assuming control of the airport, it also prioritized U.S. military flights over others and focused at first on rescuing and evacuating Americans. Médecins Sans Frontières (MSF) planes carrying surgical teams and supplies and a French aid plane carrying a field hospital were both diverted to the Dominican Republic. Some food aid spent so long at the airport that it was rotten by the time it was delivered to starving Haitians. Our armed forces play a critical role in combating extremist elements and in responding to life-threatening situations when international humanitarian actors are simply unable to operate. But the *saviour warrior* thrust must be balanced by an independent humanitarian imperative. In conflict environments in particular, the role of the military in humanitarian affairs ought to be limited to securing corridors that will allow for the safe and responsible delivery of aid by organizations knowledgeable in the field, and to training local police and security forces.

There is a simple way for the armed forces of NATO countries to responsibly contribute to aid and development globally: through United Nations peacekeeping missions. Over the past two decades, Canada's reputation as a peacekeeping nation has been in a free fall. In 1992, Canada was among the world's top ten in terms of its contribution to peacekeeping. Today it is seventy-fifth, with fewer peacekeepers deployed than Slovakia and Mali. The United States has fewer than eighty peacekeepers and ranks seventy-first, just ahead of Romania and behind Namibia. Three years into the conflict in Darfur, fewer than half of the 26,000 peacekeepers requested by the United Nations had been deployed, almost entirely from poorly equipped African Union (AU) and South Asian countries. In 2007, the AU/UN hybrid operation (UNAMID) tasked with protecting civilians in Darfur – an area the size of France, where entire villages were being attacked and their residents raped and slaughtered – issued a plea for six helicopters to move troops around under Security Council Resolution 1769. Western governments were generally unresponsive, with Ethiopia eventually providing five helicopters. The same defence departments that were spending $504 million a day on Iraq and Afghanistan couldn't muster the resources to provide even one helicopter while tens of thousands were dying.

"Peacekeeping" is presently a pejorative term in defence circles, a construct that has allegedly not kept pace with the military's post-2001 counter-insurgency and counter-terrorism role. Defence department officials also cite genuine concerns about operational mismanagement within the United Nations peacekeeping missions, and the need for greater assurances that troops are not heading into volatile situations with no reasonable means of protecting or defending themselves. In an African context, there is a valid argument to be made in favour of investing in the capacity of African Union troops to quell conflicts, rather than adding to the continent's burden of aid dependency through foreign intervention. However, reaching African Union consensus in the face of mass atrocities is subject to all the same self-interested decision making and ideological bickering that sucks the "quick" out of "response." And so conflict and post-conflict communities wait, in frustration, for those with the capacity to find the will to act, while those tasked with protecting civilians are constrained by their lack of capacity. NATO countries cannot achieve UN reform while manipulating and compounding its inefficiencies. In the meantime, the move towards military-civilian integration that includes an overarching humanitarian mandate – and aid as a "weapons system"– just adds to the confusion and contempt felt by communities plagued by war.

Despite allegations to the contrary, resistance to co-operating or collaborating with the military on the part of aid agencies is not rooted in leftist, bleeding-heart rhetoric but in international law and an understanding of what actually *works* on the ground. Defence officials repeatedly fail to grasp the importance of doing everything possible to maintain a clear distinction between aid and military efforts in unstable environments. They point to the hypocrisy of unarmed aid groups whinging about their autonomy while requiring the physical security of the troops in order to do their jobs. And they believe, with good reason, that it boosts troop morale whenever they are involved in direct humanitarian assistance. It also improves local relations. Aid has been known to reduce anti-western sentiment in traditionally hostile corners of the world. After the 2005 earthquake in Pakistan, communities that worked closely with international aid agencies and their staff showed a significant, positive change in their attitude towards foreigners, including westerners. But military-administered aid programs, by their very nature, do not foster the same level of trust, because civilians are inherently cynical about the intent and worried about being targeted as collaborators.

It's true that *no* foreign aid effort can ever be entirely uncoupled from the political and ideological objectives of donor countries, giving credence to assertions that aid can be a form of "soft" imperialism. And aid workers are not immune to their own social, cultural, and religious influences. In that sense, neither aid nor the organizations administering it can ever claim to be entirely neutral, despite their best efforts. But success and sustainability in aid and development programming require in-depth knowledge of local psychology, strong community ties, technical experience, the flexibility to modify and adapt based on rigorous evaluation and oversight, and a high degree of local acceptance and ownership.

The erosion of "humanitarian space" in war-torn environments is not a new phenomenon, nor is it unique to Iraq and Afghanistan. The 1999 NATO mission in Kosovo also saw international troops engaging in a wide range of relief activities. NATO soldiers even built camps and administered direct services to refugees, essentially subsuming the role of the United Nations High Commission for Refugees (UNHCR). This was decried by a number of credible international organizations, including Médecins Sans Frontières, who felt that it would place refugees at grave risk. The NATO refugee camps were shelled by Serb forces in Albania, Macedonia, and Montenegro. And in 2008, the U.S. Department of Defense launched its own military-humanitarian hybrid force, called AFRICOM (United States African Command). AFRICOM's mandate is to "conduct sustained security engagement through military-to-military programs, military-sponsored activities, and other military operations as directed to promote a stable and secure African environment in support of U.S. foreign policy." In practice, however, it is primarily aimed at American strategic interests in Africa, including counterterrorism activities, and at China's expanded influence in the region. AFRICOM is unabashedly transparent about its adoption of humanitarian aims as military strategy, with counterterrorism units involved in development activities such as drilling wells and rebuilding schools.

Some aid agencies have muddled things further by accepting lucrative military contracts and demonstrating a willingness to embrace an alternative military-NGO model, even though this comes at a huge price to the humanitarian movement as a whole. Over the past decade, attacks against aid workers have increased 1,000 percent, with reports of rape, violence, extortion, abduction, and killings. There are now more aid workers killed in the line of duty each year than peacekeepers. Yes, there are other realities contributing to this tragic outcome. Criminal and militant groups have seized on the emotional and financial capital of kidnapping or murdering (or both) unarmed aid workers. And aid workers themselves are pushing into more dangerous environments draped in humanitarian bunting that can no longer protect them. Still, many of those killed have simply been, through no fault of their own, in the wrong place at the wrong time. But the imperative of distinguishing between counter-insurgency, anti-terrorism military interventions and helping fractured societies recover and rebuild in times of war still remains, if only because the latter is impossible without a sustained humanitarian presence.

In Iraq, the bombing of the United Nations headquarters was merely the overture to the aggressive and ruinous aftermath of the 2003 war that has so far killed 4,754 Coalition soldiers and more than 200,000 Iraqis. Aid agencies quickly began to withdraw or limit their international staff to Jordan or Kuwait, while others took up residence in the Green Zone. The United States spent more than a quarter trillion dollars ($250 billion) during its first three years in Iraq, with very little to show for it. Meanwhile, small arms flowed freely across Iraqi borders, with financial backing from Saudi Arabia and Iran.

When the call came, I struggled to hold the receiver. "Sam? I'm sorry, did you hear me?" a friend from Baghdad repeated several times over an erratic connection. It was October 19, 2004. "Margaret was ambushed today. She's been kidnapped."

It's not possible, I thought. *She's been fighting for the Iraqi people for thirty years. She speaks Arabic fluently and is an Iraqi citizen. She openly opposed the war. Once they realize*, I assured myself, *they'll let her go.*

I learned later that her abductors had been dressed in police uniforms and stopped her car as she was being driven to the CARE office. She had offered to go with the gunmen so that her assailants would stop beating her driver and unarmed guard.

In the days that followed, there were widespread rallies in support of Margaret in Baghdad. She had helped thousands of Iraqis, and hundreds honoured her by gathering in Firdos Square carrying photographs and demanding her safe release. Even the murderous creep Abu Musab al-Zarqawi, head of Al-Qaeda in Iraq, called for Margaret to be set free. Her sisters accused the British Foreign Office of bungling the negotiations with her kidnappers, who called Margaret's husband, Tahseen Ali Hassan, and asked to be put through to embassy officials. The Foreign Office refused to speak with them in an attempt to "emphasize her Iraqi-ness." (Margaret held both U.K. and Iraqi passports.) Ironically, Margaret had been the director of the British Council Office in Baghdad before it suspended its work in the lead-up to the 1991 Gulf War.

Not long after the abduction, Margaret appeared in the first of three videotaped messages released by a group later loosely identified as the 1920 Revolutionary Brigade, one of several death squads branding themselves as "revolutionaries." She appeared worn and desperate. It is the lowest depth of human misery to witness the suffering – no, *torture* – of someone you care about and be powerless to stop it. To imagine, worst of all, her family watching as she bargained and begged, then surrendered to the indignity of those final moments. Especially Margaret Hassan, whose name was synonymous with the struggle of the Iraqi people, with exposing the injustices they had endured, and whose influence was so strongly felt precisely because she bridged the cultural divide. Margaret was not someone who recoiled: she could not be intimidated, or manipulated, or placated. She was compassionate, but exacting – even, at times, predictably obstinate.

"Please help me," she cries on the message filmed by her captors and broadcast worldwide. "These might be my last hours. Please help me. Please tell the British people to ask Mr. Blair to take the troops out of Iraq and not to bring them here in Baghdad. That's why people like Mr. Bigley and myself are being caught and maybe we will die. I will die like Mr. Bigley. Please, please, I beg of you." Kenneth Bigley was a British engineer who was kidnapped and murdered less than two weeks before Margaret's abduction.

In the second tape, which was never broadcast, Margaret is forced to read a bogus statement, confessing that she "worked with the occupation forces" by giving information to American troops.

On November 16, CARE issued a press release announcing the existence of a third video, this one showing Margaret's execution. Al Jazeera, which received the tape, refused to broadcast it, explaining that it was too distressing. The video shows Margaret standing blindfolded in an empty room with her head bowed. A man with a scarf hiding his face approaches from behind holding a handgun. He squeezes the trigger, and there is a click as the gun misfires. Margaret does not move. The man leaves and then reappears. He fires the gun again. This time Margaret utters a slight cry then falls backwards onto a plastic sheet on the floor. Margaret's body has not yet been found.

———

ON THE WAY TO BASRA, in the south of Iraq, in a town called Al Qurnah, where the waters of the Tigris and Euphrates touch one another, is a grassless park. At the rivers' edge, shirtless boys gut the day's catch while women scrub lathered toddlers. The park, which contains a single leafless tree, is walled against the encroaching waters and the area's wild dogs, which nevertheless defecate all along the exterior. The park itself is unimpressive, but the view is magnificent: the waters are shallow but expansive, disappearing into vast marshes that at one time extended to the indigenous Marsh Arabs, before Saddam drained and destroyed their delicate habitat.

Al Qurnah is believed by some Christians, Muslims, and Jews to be the ancient site of the Garden of Eden. Whether you are biblically inclined or not, it is an extraordinary experience to place yourself within thousands of years of civilization. "Adam's Tree" is a withering eucalyptus blackened at the base by fire, hollow and filled with concrete. There is no canopy – only a few broken limbs too high and thick to be easily cut and carried home for firewood. Before the Iran-Iraq war, the site attracted large numbers of foreign tourists, but it seems unlikely to ever earn such attention again, even in the absence of war. Children, mostly street kids, play and sleep under the tree, safe from the dogs that routinely maul them.

An elderly man approaches and introduces himself as the groundskeeper. He sentimentally reflects on the attraction's headier days, and carries faded pictures of bell-bottomed tourists against a sun-bleached terrain. The children run and tug at one another, cajoling the old man for bread or money. He has neither. I ask him how the tree died.

"The foreigners who visited," he replies, "would break off a small branch or leaf as a souvenir. They all wanted a piece of Adam's Tree to keep for themselves. It is a loss that can never be recovered."

CHAPTER 4

PAVED WITH GOOD INTENTIONS

> Every morning in Africa a gazelle awakens knowing it
> must run today faster than the fastest lion or it will be eaten.
> Every morning a lion awakens knowing it must outrun the slowest
> gazelle or it will starve. It matters not whether you are a gazelle
> or a lion, when the sun rises you had better be running.
>
> AFRICAN PROVERB, UNKNOWN ORIGIN

It's a common enough sight in West Africa. A young aid worker, ponytailed and baseball-capped, standing barefoot at the side of the road while children hawk overripe mangos.

"You buy, Missy, you buy?"

"No, thank you."

"You give me pen, Missy, I go to school. You have pen, Missy?"

"Not today," I tell them, holding up empty palms.

"Coca-Cola, Missy? Please. I am thirsty."

"Can't you see, boys? I don't even have *shoes*," I say, and they laugh. The older boys, the ten- and twelve-year-olds, wear discarded tour shirts and other pop-culture flashbacks rejected by suburban American teenagers before well-meaning parents stuffed them into charity drop boxes: "Don't Worry, Be Happy," "Choose Life," "Thompson Twins."

An emaciated, naked, and clearly deranged adolescent boy is dancing behind us, rhythmically chanting and rubbing his hands along his thighs. "War make him crazy," the tallest boy offers when he sees me look over, clasping his hands over his head. "He soldier. Too much brown-brown. Whoah,"* he whistles, as if to emphasize the point. "He kill many people. Now he always singing and dancing like he happy. He don't know what he done. But no one else forget."

I'm in Liberia on the margins of a small town, having just crawled out of the window of a United Nations Land Cruiser wedged door-high in mud, my sneakers somewhere under the back seat. It's almost one year after Charles Taylor, the former rebel leader of the National Patriotic Front of Liberia, became president. During the previous seven years, Taylor had waged a catastrophic civil war, recruiting and abducting Liberian children in his quest to overthrow the country's post-independence government. In September 1990, a rebel group led by Taylor's former ally Prince Johnson captured and murdered then-president Samuel Doe. (With a camera rolling, the group tortured and mutilated Doe: the video, which was seen around the world, shows them cutting off his ear while Johnson stands in the background sipping a beer.) In the war that ensued, some 250,000 people died, fully 10 percent of the population, and more than 800,000 became refugees. According to UNICEF, 6,000 of the rebel troops were child soldiers. One of Taylor's election slogans declared: "He killed my Ma, he killed my Pa, but I will vote for him."

As with other despots, Taylor co-opted tribalism and ethnicity to manufacture support under a nationalist banner for a war from which he stood to singularly profit. During the nineteenth

---

* "Brown-brown" is a mixture of cocaine and smokeless gunpowder that was given to child soldiers in West Africa.

century, freed slaves living in the United States (as well as many who had migrated to Canada) were relocated to West Africa by the government-sponsored American Colonization Society, where they established the Republic of Liberia. It was marketed as a progressive move that would enable African Americans to "return" to their homeland and own property, even though most had lived in the United States for generations. Instead, it was a coercive program, decried by anti-slavery groups, that yielded disastrous results. Upon landing in this unfamiliar tropical environment, many of them became ill or died after contracting diseases such as malaria and yellow fever, while others returned to the United States penniless. Those who stayed clashed with the indigenous population, attempting, with Shakespearian poignancy, to "civilize" them while fighting with them for land ownership. By 1870, although these immigrants (calling themselves Americo-Liberians) made up less than 5 percent of the population, they had established what the historian Morten Bøås calls "an apartheid state." For more than a century, he writes, this small group of elites "dominated every aspect of political and economic life for their own benefit."

Some 120 years later, Taylor (despite rumours of his own Americo-Liberian lineage) appealed to Liberia's indigenous groups, perversely convincing them that they'd been subjugated by the descendants of freed American slaves for too long, and it was time to reclaim Liberia for "the Africans." His criminal activity was financed by the illicit trading of natural resources, particularly the diamonds mined in his own country and those smuggled from neighbouring Sierra Leone, which also descended into a brutal war lasting from 1991 to 2002.

"Lurking beneath the surface of every society, including ours," writes former war correspondent Chris Hedges in his brilliant and intrepid book *War Is a Force That Gives Us Meaning*, "is the passionate yearning for a nationalist cause that exalts us, the kind that war alone is able to deliver. It reduces and at times erases the anxiety of individual consciousness." This weakness in human nature is exploited by war-makers like Taylor all around the world, with religion predictably added as an accelerant.

I ask the boys if they'll help me find wood to place under the tires to get some traction. Now I'm on the hook for those Cokes. My driver, Moses, is shouting into the radio for another UN vehicle to come from our destination, Voinjama, to collect us before nightfall. With large sections of the single-lane dirt road washed out, it would be at least three hours before someone arrived, and assuming the other side was passable. We both knew it would take less time for word to spread of an unarmed driver, a $60,000 United Nations vehicle, and a white woman trapped in the middle of the bush. (Fortunately, this was before Africa became one of the world's fastest-growing mobile phone markets, so we still had time to review our options.)

Moses is furious now. "I told that *Nigerian*," he fumes, meaning our logistician in Monrovia, "that rains come *early* to the north. I drive. I know. Now we wait for ambush?" He is more visibly alarmed than I am, and we both know why. In the event of an ambush, which commonly occur on Liberia's back roads, our attackers will most likely kill him. They will try to extort money from me, but eventually they'll let me go. It is rare for Liberians, despite committing heinous misdeeds against one another, to kidnap and murder foreigners. Taylor is seeking legitimacy and aid money from wealthy nations to prop up his government and assure his authority, and it is widely rumoured that he has ordered his combatants to leave foreign aid workers unharmed.

I propose to Moses that he carry a walkie-talkie and go on foot to see whether the road ahead is clear. It's a futile exercise, because around every blind corner lurks another. But if trouble does show up and he's not in the vicinity, I reason, perhaps no one will waste time looking for him. Moses refuses. He won't leave me alone with the boys.

After an hour or so, the radio receiver crackles. Our rescue vehicle from Voinjama already has a flat. All other UN vehicles are even farther away. The boys have collected logs, which we push blindly into the bog and attempt to wedge under the tires. It becomes a frenzy of limbs, mud, and riotous laughter as we all slip and sink into the muck. Moses instructs me to get into the driver's seat and put the vehicle into low gear while he pushes and rocks from behind with the largest of the boys. It lurches to one side, then inches forward. The wheels start spinning. Moses shouts for me to stop so the logs can be repositioned.

We are making modest progress when we hear a truck clamouring towards us. From the laboured sound, the bottom is about to drop out of it. I can see a group of young men in dark colours standing behind the steel cab of a flatbed truck, gripping the top as it frenetically bounces and dips towards us. My hands shake, but my strong urge to flee is tempered by a cowardly fatalism – if I run they will give chase, and if I hide they will know where to find me.

The smallest boys scatter, while Moses and the others have a hurried conversation in Bassa, one of the local languages. Moses grabs the car radio. "Echo One, Echo One. This is Charlie Four. Unknown vehicle approaching. Possibly armed. Over."

Static fills the line, then, "This is Echo One. Message received. Over. "

There is odd comfort in security rituals at precisely the moment when they matter least: they give the illusion of control when you are at your most helpless. Our delusional former child soldier is still dancing.

The young men jump from the truck as the driver gears down, his brakes wincing against the rusted frame. No guns. I'm so relieved I am suddenly nauseous. They take stock of our situation – a middle-aged Liberian in a blue driver's uniform, a teenage-looking white woman, and three scrawny boys, all caked in mud – and start laughing. "So," says the truck driver as he steps from his vehicle, "this is why the UN get nothing done for the people of Liberia?"

I smile. "Well, we foreigners think we can control nature, but Africans know better, huh?" I'm still not sure how this is going to go. He says something in Bassa to Moses, who nods agreeably and responds, and the men chuckle.

"I get my chains," the driver announces, as his colleagues wade into the muck to assess our front bumper.

They loop the chains through the frame of our vehicle then hook them to a hitch at the back of the truck. The men push forcefully as Moses grips the wheel and our vehicle rises from the mud. We shake hands and snap fingers – as is the local custom – and then I reach into the back of the Land Cruiser and open all of our provisions. The boys get their Cokes. The members of the truck crew stuff instant soup mix and granola bars into their pockets. They had been on their way home from delivering lumber to an NGO in one of the Sierra Leonean refugee camps, but had been delayed because of road conditions. They will now be sleeping here until it proves possible to cross.

Once we are moving again, I ask Moses what the truck driver said to him.

"He say it dangerous for a young white girl to be out here, and ask me why we driving to Voinjama this time of year."

"What did you tell him?"

"Because of a know-nothing Nigerian."

———

I WAS IN LIBERIA to lead a joint national review for UNICEF and the United Nations Development Fund for Women (UNIFEM) on maternal and child health in Liberia. The findings and recommendations would form part of the government's operational strategy, as well as a UN appeal for the country as it sought to re-establish itself under a new president. Whether I held anything less than absolute disdain for the murderous former rebel leader and his patronage-appointed thugs was not at issue. It is the role of UN agencies in fragile states to provide support to and coordinate with recognized governments (in this case, a democratically elected one), however corrupt, opportunistic, or ineffective they may be. NGOs, on the other hand, operate in their own spheres, with accountabilities to external stakeholders (foreign donors and governments), not national ones, except voluntarily. It is a chronic tension in the aid community, one I constantly struggled with while working in Liberia.

"How can you stand to know you are propping up that asshole?" was an accusation frequently levied at me by NGO colleagues, as I was the sole UN employee among my group of friends. We'd gather for drinks a few times a week at the Lebanese-run Mamba Point Hotel in Monrovia – a popular landing with expats. It didn't take long for me to dread such conversations, if only because of my own mixed convictions on the subject. I understood why most of my officemates preferred to spend their evenings alone in their gated UN compounds. My usual response was: "And what will happen to your programs when you eventually run out of funding? What then? What capacity are you leaving behind?" Along with, "Oh god, not *this* again."

My mandate in Liberia was an ambitious, months-long review involving travel to remote areas. I was desperately short of information upon which to base my assessment. Government health records had been looted or destroyed during Doe's overthrow. Apart from Médecins Sans Frontières (MSF), very few agencies bothered to track epidemiological trends that are essential for knowing, for example, whether a catastrophic measles outbreak is looming. At the time of my trip to Voinjama, my Liberian research partner, a medical doctor named Musa, was bedridden with malaria. I had a long list of hospitals and clinics to visit in the area, and several days of interviews with relief workers.

My first stop in Voinjama, though, was the market, where essential no-cost medicines were reportedly being sold for profit, still in their UNICEF bottles. The suspected source was a UNICEF-funded clinic a few kilometres outside of town, and I had received precise instructions from headquarters – given that I was making the twelve-hour journey "anyway" – to verify the allegations and issue a written warning to the person responsible. It was relatively rare for senior staff to venture outside the capital, and they were trying to off-load the problem to the obnoxiously eager new kid. I wasn't in a position to refuse, nor was I inclined to. If someone was, in effect, stealing medicines intended for sick children and pregnant women who might die without them – well, in my view, this was reprehensible. That person needed to be confronted, and I was prepared to do it.

Upon arriving in the market, it became obvious that this wasn't a simple case of a few pocketed bottles of acetaminophen. In fact, apart from random bunches of withering cassava leaves and fly-covered, dried fish heads, residents did not appear to be selling anything *but* relief supplies pilfered from dozens of international aid agencies. Bags of maize and wheat, oral rehydration therapy, school kits, high-protein biscuits, and plastic sheeting were all conspicuously for sale in their original, branded packaging.

A certain amount of "reassignment" of donated goods is unavoidable, and even accepted as normal. Organizations running food distribution programs in unstable environments often factor such losses into their calculations when planning their shipments. While they may not admit it, some groups running distribution programs have even been known to send shipments of food to armed groups as part of a deal to ensure their civilian supplies aren't looted. And only the custodians of imperialism would presume that impoverished families had neither the right nor the reason to resell handouts they felt they could do without (or trade for something they truly needed). But this was a very different problem. This was something systematic, as if aid was rapidly becoming the *only* economy in Voinjama.

I was able to determine that a physician's assistant (PA) at our clinic was indeed the primary supplier of UNICEF medications to the local market. Moses and I set off to confront him. On the way over, I questioned the usefulness of issuing a written warning. There was no one in Voinjama to do follow-up spot checks. It would make more sense, I reasoned, just to fire him outright.

The clinic was deep in the bush and we pulled in behind a long line of patients awaiting assessment, some writhing on blankets. My anger deepened. I introduced myself to the PA, whose name was Jacob, and before launching into my accusations I asked to see the storeroom. Better, I thought, to have this conversation beside his empty shelves.

"As you will see," he said, unlocking the door, "there is never enough medicine. I have asked UNICEF many times to increase our supplies. You see the people waiting? This clinic is very busy." There were still several unopened boxes of iron tablets and vitamin A, and a reasonable but thinning number of medications used to treat the most common complaints like cough, malaria, dysentery, parasites, rashes, and sexually transmitted infections.

I responded that I'd been in the market earlier and knew he was selling the drugs. He was unabashed when he heard this; if anything, he appeared to find me amusing.

"How did you get here today?" Jacob asked.

"Please explain to me," I replied, "how drugs from this clinic are ending up in the market."

"I am explaining it to you," he said. "You came in that nice car. New car. And do you get paid?"

"Of course I get paid. And so do you. Which is why you have no right to sell medications meant for *them*." I pointed through the barred window to the crowd outside.

"Yes, I get paid." He was now furious with me and his English started to break. "I get paid food for work.* A woman like you come and say, 'You do this work, we give you food every month.' Not money. *Food*. My children are hungry, so I say yes. I work all day and sleep here, because too far to go home. When my food come, I take my bicycle and go home, one day each way. But for three months, my food don't come. No one from UN come. You the first in three months."

---

* Food-for-work programs, such as the WFP's Food for Assets program, offer staples like rice and maize in exchange for labour on projects such as building roads, bridges, hospitals, schools, ports, and other infrastructure.

"I didn't know, Jacob. I'm sorry."

"No one know because no one ask." He starts to weep. "I sell the medicines, so I can feed my family and treat my patients. And you ask me, is this *right*?"

I didn't issue the warning. I assured Jacob I'd speak to the appropriate people back in Monrovia and try to resolve the situation.

"And you bought that?" asked an acquaintance, as I relayed Jacob's story to The Assembled at the Mamba Point bar a few weeks later. "Shit. He played you. Have you even asked WFP to check their records?" Such recriminations were regrettably common, inseparable from the "us" and "them" rhetoric of Liberia's NGO culture. I had indeed followed up with WFP (the World Food Programme), who confirmed that the refugee crisis in neighbouring Sierra Leone, as well as the poor road conditions, had resulted in shortfalls in food-for-work programs. They were attempting to rectify the situation. Nevertheless, each day I found it harder to shake the feeling that I was part of a sector that was rapidly squandering its moral legitimacy.

Aid is an imperfect response to a violently imperfect world. That aid can be manipulated to prop up corrupt, oppressive regimes or become a form of political and cultural imperialism is not even in debate. But I reject the assertion that aid is the primary problem, or that impoverished and war-ravaged people would be a lot better off if we relied solely on the *noblesse oblige* of free market economics. I hope I have already provided compelling reasons, best exemplified by the widespread human rights abuses taking place in eastern Congo, as to why corporate-driven economic development in struggling nations is not the panacea some portray it to be. It is equally misguided to assume that aid stifles social unrest by producing "dependency" drones who won't question their own oppression until the taps run dry. On the contrary, aid can be enormously beneficial in improving education and health, strengthening governance, and promoting social stability. Aid has the potential to be of tremendous value in tackling systemic injustices and inequities, and in curbing deaths from war, famine, and natural disasters. The challenge is in knowing which factors contribute to the various sides of this equation.

The origins of modern humanitarian action can be traced to Henry Dunant, the founder of the International Committee of the Red Cross. Horrified by the atrocities of war in Europe, he compelled European nations to sign the treaty of the First Geneva Convention in 1864 in order to recognize the neutrality of wounded combatants and the medics who assisted them. After World War I, additional aid groups appeared – notably Save the Children, founded in the United Kingdom in 1919 – and ushered in the current model of the independent and operational NGO. World War II provided the catalyst for the next phase: Oxfam was formed in 1942, CARE in 1945, and World Vision (a Christian aid group) in 1950. The United Nations and its agencies were also born during this time.

By the 1960s, international instruments relating to prisoners and civilians in war, refugees, and human rights were in place, and mechanisms for transporting relief goods and food aid became more efficient. When the Nigerian government went to war against the rebel state of Biafra in 1967, people in the West were shocked by the photos and stories of Biafran children starving to death. I was born a few years after this crisis, but I still remember my grandmother threatening to send my dinner to the "Children of Biafra" whenever I rejected her cooking as a child. My cousins and I had no idea where Biafra was, but assumed it had to be a fairly wretched place if they were being mailed Nanna's soggy Brussels sprouts. (I only got away with saying "Perhaps that's why they're starving" once.)

As the governments of western countries struggle with declining public confidence and voter apathy (most pronounced among those under thirty years of age), NGOs appeal to their sense of effectuality and social responsibility. Participation in NGOs also offers a "safe" alternative to traditional forms of protest – such as public demonstrations and petitions – for the middle majority discomfited by police barricades or cynical about their capacity to change government policy. I am encouraged by the growing number of people who approach me wanting to volunteer or align themselves with a cause. The more disengaged we become from government, the more attractive NGOs become. It's a reciprocal relationship that leaves aid agencies and those who support them feeling empowered and energized. But in a more generic sense, the rise of NGOs, domestic and international, allows governments of both developed and developing countries to off-load health and social programs (and to some extent foreign diplomacy) to a cabal of vested interests. Over time, this creates huge regulatory gaps and degrades the role of government, a pattern that is exaggerated in developing countries. "What is my government doing for me?" is quickly replaced by, "Where are the NGOs while our people are suffering?" NGOs themselves contribute to such expectations by hyper-branding every crisis and overplaying their hand.

There are, however, ways to avoid such outcomes. It starts with decreasing the profile of international aid organizations at the field level, while simultaneously increasing the capacity and credibility of local civil society groups. But this takes time and investment, and interferes with the high-velocity, boots-on-the-ground, saving-lives ethos of aid groups that speaks to their donors back home and therefore brings the highest financial return.

For the most part, the aid workers I have met and the organizations they represent are taking bold steps to reduce poverty and human suffering, and to advance human rights around the world. The majority work long hours for far less than their skills and qualifications might earn in any other line of work, and often at great personal risk. But we are also part of a sector that clings to models of humanitarian action – some new, some old – that deserve careful scrutiny if we are ever to achieve our common goal.

The biggest and best known international NGOs in the world (MSF, World Vision, CARE, Save the Children, Oxfam, International Committee of the Red Cross, Catholic Relief Services, and PLAN) share a common trait. They are either exclusively or significantly engaged in emergency relief, which means they have to move quickly to be at the front of any natural disaster. Public reaction to such crises is remarkably swift. Less than three weeks after the 2010 earthquake in Haiti, for example, donors had pledged well over half a billion dollars. This places inordinate pressure on relief groups to accomplish three "Ps" in the wake of any disaster: be present, be prominent, and be proprietary.

The third P, proprietary, refers to two disaster-related phenomena. During an emergency public appeal, agencies must distinguish themselves and convince donors why they are best suited for the job. A relief agency will typically implore: "Give to (insert name of agency)! We're on the ground saving lives!" These messages are further lined with a smattering of qualifiers intended to debunk the competition, such as "Present in (insert name of hapless country) for thirty years," or "fifty years" . . . and so it goes. The second phenomenon happens at the field level. In the cluttered humanitarian landscape following a disaster and under pressure to show results, organizations must quickly claim "their" territory or risk being unable to fulfill their mandate and their promise to donors, and losing their access to equally lucrative international government grants. It's typical for aid groups in emergencies to attach their names to displaced people's camps, or even whole areas: "the World Vision Camp," "the Save Camp," "the PLAN Camp," and so on. These are normally identical in every way, except for the logos. The circus aspect to this may have reached its pinnacle during the Haiti earthquake, when the number of international agencies claiming to be leading the recovery defied common sense.

All of this also drives the competition for local partner agencies and staff, the best of whom are aggressively courted by the organizations with the deepest pockets, driving up costs (especially salaries), sabotaging long-standing relationships, and creating expectations that are impossible to manage over the long term. And the difference between the response to natural and "man-made" disasters is absolutely staggering.* The 2004 South Asian tsunami killed an estimated 300,000 people and received about $1 billion in donations, while the Haiti earthquake claimed some 200,000 lives (though more recent assessments by the U.S. Agency for International Development have revised the death toll to between 46,000 and 85,000 people) and attracted $1.4 billion in private funds.

---

* While I'm usually loath to use "man-made" in place of the more inclusive "human," let's not fool ourselves: civil wars are, more often than not, *man*-made.

International governments also pledged a further $5.8 billion for tsunami relief and $9.9 billion to reconstruction efforts in Haiti. Let us avoid, for the time being, wading into an analysis of how much of those funds are still unspent (in the case of the tsunami) or undelivered (in the case of Haiti). Almost all of the deaths from these two catastrophes took place on the first day, without warning. By comparison, the war in the Democratic Republic of Congo killed in excess of 5 million people over eight years, with up to 45,000 people dying monthly in its violent aftermath. Similarly, the war in Darfur, Sudan, has killed an estimated 300,000 people and displaced 2 million since 2003. In both cases, there was warning after warning after warning. Yet, the total amount of international humanitarian assistance to Congo and Sudan (including Darfur) during the peak years of these humanitarian crises paled in comparison to the amount committed to Haiti, which was the largest appeal in history. There is a sharp, incontrovertible stigma attached to war that places a value judgment on, for example, the corpses of three-year-olds – a tragic reality that is reflected in patterns of aid distribution. How, when, and to whom aid is bestowed is therefore influenced by a variety of factors, some rational but many not. And compounding it all is, on the one hand, a growing monopoly of the aid sector by ever-larger organizations that function (both practically and philosophically) like multinational corporations and, on the other, a reflexive boom in the number of recreational humanitarians seeking to bypass those bureaucracies.

Consider Haiti. Within three weeks of the January 12, 2010, earthquake there were countless international organizations on the ground, along with 22,000 troops and 8,500 United Nations peacekeepers, who'd suffered a serious blow with the loss of their head of mission and 102 personnel. I arrived in late February to follow up on a program that War Child had begun developing prior to the earthquake. In partnership with local NGOs, it focused on sexual and gender-based violence and the legal representation of girls and women. With over 1.5 million displaced Haitians living in squats and haphazard tented areas, cases of rape and sexual exploitation were increasing rapidly, the Ministry of Justice had collapsed, and the need for highly specialized programming was enormous.

As the images of a destroyed Port-au-Prince and its distraught citizens overwhelmed news outlets, the migration of NGOs and the aggressive jockeying for media positioning began. In what can only be characterized as a media coup, some journalists embedded with relief workers. Other newscasts included reports submitted directly by agency representatives as they flocked from the Dominican Republic towards the unfolding drama. It became so problematic that the Society of Professional Journalists (SPJ) eventually issued a press release cautioning journalists against becoming part of the story they were reporting. All of those visitors also had to be fed, housed, and equipped with supplies. Most goods were procured locally, adding to their scarcity and driving up costs. CNN reportedly bought up most of the rooms at Le Plaza, one of the few hotels left standing in the city.

It is difficult to know which variables contributed most to what Haitians call "*la République des ONG,*" the Republic of NGOs: the country's proximity and close ties to North America; the horrifying visual impact of the devastation and ruined lives; the preponderance of NGOs and faith-based groups already operating in Haiti; the frenzied media response; or the sheer scale of the disaster. Nevertheless, the relief onslaught was unprecedented for a country Haiti's size.

While United Nations agencies in Haiti hand-picked their most senior and experienced staff from around the world, thousands of other self-declared relief workers arrived with little to no knowledge of disaster management and few tangible skills. They were not doctors or nurses, or water and sanitation engineers, or logisticians, or any other form of expert who could help with a coordinated, effective response. Nor were they there, as the UN was, to rebuild the government or support its devastated civil service (large numbers of whom died in buildings that failed to meet minimum engineering and safety standards). Rather, they were an odd combination of gawkers and do-gooders, proselytizers and community groups, who'd been unable to resist the urge to *do something*. Many of these individuals could be seen in their conspicuously matching T-shirts, on "missions," walking the streets of Port-au-Prince or riding on the back of Hiluxes, looking for a place to begin. In one extreme case, ten members of an American Baptist group were caught smuggling thirty-three Haitian children across the Dominican Republic border. They called it a rescue. Most of the children, who were presumed to be orphans, turned out to have parents.

Coordination among NGOs is virtually anathema to an industry that thrives on its autonomy while being ruled by its competitiveness. But the problems in Haiti far exceeded the norm, in no small part because of all the inexperienced groups on the ground. Consider the following scenario: In a mid-sized North American town, a handful of well-intentioned individuals collect supplies such as shoes, clothing, blankets, and infant formula. These they sort in a friend's warehouse until they can box them up and accompany them onto a commercial flight ("It's for the children of Haiti!"). They arrive in Port-au-Prince gleefully eager to start. They choose a location and hand out the goods, sending multiple emails home declaring their trip a success and thanking all who contributed. They leave elated by the experience. Except that one of the worst things you can do in an environment with limited drinking water, and even less public education about the risks, is provide a direct gateway for cholera and dysentery to enter the open mouths of babies who were most likely being successfully breastfed. It is gross negligence. And yet, through the "gift" of formula, it happened.

Such feel-good exercises also spawn civil unrest, as displaced people in other camps demand to know why they are not receiving the same level of benefits. This is in addition to the negative impact that such distributions have on community markets and other income-generating activities, which are undermined every time western surplus goods flood local economies.

Different scenario, same predictable results: A group arrives ready to rebuild and refurbish an orphanage in Haiti. (The country has hundreds of these institutions – probably more per capita than any other nation in the world.) They've conducted their own emergency appeal in high schools and Legion halls, promising accountability because they're going to do the work themselves. The orphanage is rebuilt, stocked, and opened for business. With so many of Haiti's orphanages under rubble, their tiny occupants and volunteer staff dead or grieving, and with many more children alone and in need, it seems crass and insensitive to criticize such magnanimity. Except that destitute families are now surrendering their children to the orphanage, because they know they will at least be fed and have a comfortable place to sleep. Meanwhile, community leaders, who were not consulted on the project, ask why the funds were not spent instead on ensuring that families had the means and the opportunity to care for their children – or the children of dead relatives – themselves. Every major study on this issue has found that institutionalizing children is harmful to their physical, emotional, and psychological development. That's why orphanages no longer exist in North America.

As part of its aid priorities, Haiti needs to begin phasing out its overflowing orphanages and reuniting children with extended family members. This can be accomplished by investing, through community-based networks, in the economic self-sufficiency of families and in strengthening local support systems such as school-based nutrition and after-care programs, and by improving women's reproductive health services. I spoke to several people who assured me orphanages are "part of Haiti's social fabric." This is utter nonsense; they are institutions established and funded almost exclusively by foreigners. It doesn't matter if the orphanage has been there for forty years under the leadership of the most benevolent Order of Nuns ever to grace the planet. Bad development doesn't improve with age. Orphanages are symptomatic of a failed system of aid, one that should have been critically reviewed as part of a broader, national child welfare and protection strategy before so many of them were feverishly rebuilt.

The myth of humanitarian assistance and aid more generally is that there is a simple linear relationship between good intentions and improved lives. Even credible international organizations have unwittingly aided violence and contributed to human suffering. After the Rwandan genocide, for example, hundreds of thousands of Hutus, many of whom had instigated the slaughter, fled to Goma, Zaire, into the waiting arms of aid agencies. They used the refugee camps as safe havens while they regrouped and rearmed, before launching attacks on the new Tutsi-led government of Rwanda. The *génocidaires* knew precisely what they were doing, and aid groups were unwitting accomplices.

Yet none of this is readily identifiable from the photos of smiling children warmly embracing their foreign saviours. Haiti and many other impoverished regions of the world are plagued by misspent altruism. In Haiti, as in many other complex human-itarian environments, responsibility for coordination following the earthquake fell to the United Nations through the formation of thematically based "cluster groups." These are voluntary associations designed to identify needs, avoid duplication, and promote collaboration, and they are used in many emergencies. Some cluster groups (Health was especially popular) attracted hundreds of representatives from the aid community, many of whom did not speak French – the country's principal language of writing, school instruction, and official business. (Virtually everyone in Haiti also speaks Creole.) In order to accommodate the foreign majority, most of the cluster meetings were held in English, further marginalizing most of the Haitians present. The meetings were, with rare exceptions, unwieldy. In short order they were being called "cluster fucks."

The Haitian government, long blighted by corruption and mismanagement, was in a state of total paralysis. The American military patrolled the streets of Port-au-Prince. In a country with more U.S. troops per capita than Afghanistan, America's strategic interests would not be overlooked. Bill Clinton was appointed UN Special Envoy for Haiti – despite his govern-ment's policies of the 1990s being fingered (among other sordid accusations) for devastating Haiti's rice industry, a mistake for which he apologized in 2010. As announcements of humanitarian assistance to Haiti were made by governments around the world (few with actual cheques attached), the inevitable question, once the emergency phase had concluded, was, "What now?"

There were many possible answers: democratic reform and improved governance; infrastructure and economic development; investment in health, education (including the development of a national curriculum), and agriculture; reforestation and environmental clean-up; job creation, particularly for youth, and skills training; disarmament; housing; law and order . . . the list goes on and on. All of these goals were equally valid and pressing, but progress on all fronts would prove slow and strained. Why? Certainly, the ongoing incompetence of the Haitian government was one major factor. The other was the dysfunction embedded in aid itself.

The rapid growth of the aid sector has led to an onslaught of personal projects and NGO start-ups directed by individuals with no relevant experience. The humanitarian sector is increasingly overrun by these assorted groups, who maintain low levels of development literacy and presume that "every little bit helps." It does not. This is one of the regrettable consequences of NGO mass marketing, in which hands-on experiences have become popular social currency.

At the same time, larger NGOs lack the incentive to coordinate, which is both time-consuming and constraining and interferes with the "proprietary" imperative critical to fundraising. Big, well-funded organizations are rarely in the mood to appease or take direction from national governments or anyone else. They'll co-operate only when it suits their interests and serves their mandate. They alone decide when, who, and how to assist, and for what length of time. This is one of the reasons why it is common to see independent hospitals and clinics run by relief groups, staffed with a full complement of western doctors, many years after the original crisis has passed.

Another major flaw lies in the way aid is allocated. In the 2005 Paris Declaration on Aid Effectiveness, donor nations resolved to increase the amount of aid they provided directly to recipient governments, rather than relying on NGOs and UN agencies to act as intermediaries. This, in theory, would allow these countries to improve their own internal capacity and to be credited for the delivery of social programs, providing greater assurances of political stability. But this logic is confounded by the presence of so many corrupt, illegitimate, and despotic regimes lording over countries at the bottom of the Human Development Index. In these contexts, cheques from donor countries are more likely to be cashed on weapons arsenals and maintaining totalitarian rule than on vaccination programs and primary schools.

A year after the Haitian earthquake, less than 30 percent of the aid funding that was pledged had actually been disbursed. Even though international government donors were right to press "pause" on direct assistance to Haiti's government in the wake of widespread electoral fraud and an unstable political climate, there are mechanisms to support the recovery through other means, such as by strengthening civil society groups. But when funding is consistently delayed, humanitarian efforts stagnate, making it much harder to move from relief to development at precisely the moment when such a transition is urgently needed. This is the Catch-22 of delivering aid in fragile states: limited funds are continuously allocated to short-term relief projects, because the conditions are not deemed conducive to longer-term development programs. Yet by the time the conditions *are* deemed appropriate, donors have lost interest or have moved on to new priorities.

Two things happen at the field level when relief programs

overshadow development initiatives for prolonged periods. One, communities become less self-sufficient and resilient; and, two, stability remains ever more elusive. It's possible to avoid this, but not without concerted effort on the part of aid agencies themselves.

The organizations most effective at mobilizing both public and government support are those primarily identified as "emergency responders." The Canadian Red Cross, for example, raised in excess of $360 million after the 2004 tsunami, almost double the organization's entire revenues from the previous year. The $54 million collected by Médecins Sans Frontières (MSF) for the same crisis ended up exceeding what they felt they needed for relief activities, and in an admirable display of transparency the organization announced it no longer required donations for this specific crisis, but would gratefully reallocate to other neglected regions. It was a bold, unprecedented move and, encouragingly, less than 1 percent of the funds were returned because donors requested a refund.

At the same time, the Canadian government announced that it would match public donations to registered charities, dollar for dollar. Such funding incentives have become routine in Canada, despite their inherent flaws. To qualify for the matching funds, organizations needed to have experience in disaster relief and had to be able to demonstrate relevant experience in more than one country. That's reasonable enough, but the problem was that media outlets were then provided with an initial list of pre-approved organizations, which consolidated donations and aid funding around a small number of large agencies. The criteria ended up excluding smaller but highly effective grassroots Canadian organizations whose *only* mandate was to work with communities within one of the affected countries, and who had devoted decades to the task. These were organizations such as the Butterfly Peace Garden, which carried out specialized and internationally recognized psychosocial programming with traumatized Sri Lankan children, with the kind of local credibility, knowledge, and access that large international agencies could only dream of. These grassroots organizations could apply to be added to the list once they had proven their eligibility, but by that time most donors had already sent their cheques to the Red Cross.

Similar problems plagued the 2010 Haiti matched-funding program. In the case of Haiti, however, the government of Canada announced that it would match donations to a general fund, which it would then disburse to agencies at its discretion. The first disbursement was to a for-profit corporation in Alberta for an untendered contract of $12 million to build temporary offices for the Haitian government.

The status quo, therefore, emphasizes short-term initiatives over longer-term strategies aimed at reducing dependence and strengthening community organizations within developing countries. This relief impulse further stifles innovation within the aid sector by continuously rewarding an elite group of large aid agencies, and those with political ties.

I'm not suggesting we "take a pass" when disaster strikes in other parts of the world. On the contrary, that is precisely the time to demonstrate the compassion and consideration that binds us together as human beings. But when moved to give, in the face of tragedy beyond our borders, consider also making a donation, post-dated to the following year, to support long-term development.

If aid is starting to sound like big business, that's because it is. The annual budget of World Vision's U.S. section alone is more than $1 billion. The American Red Cross brought in $2.6 billion in 2016 on top of the nearly $1 billion the agency held in assets. In Canada, the non-profit sector is worth some $80 billion, almost 8 percent of the country's GDP – larger than the automotive and manufacturing industries combined (the largest 1 percent of non-profits and charities in Canada receive 60 percent of the revenues). Worldwide, NGOs employ an estimated 9 million people and have a combined annual budget of well over $1 trillion.

The infrastructure required to support large organizations that rely heavily on expatriate field staff is significant, from salaries and vehicles to security, insurance, and accommodation. Organizations with a relief mandate must be capable of expediently deploying teams to augment those already on the ground, and must have the logistical network to move supplies. It is a formidable task, and one that is justifiably expensive. Relief operations demand specialized knowledge and pre-existing capacity.

In the same way, development programming is also highly technical, and to be both effective and appropriate requires rigorous consultation and evaluation, and must be driven from the ground up. Sustainable development is an iterative process, one that questions itself and is constantly evolving. A successful project places local communities and organizations at the centre of that process in the search for answers. Every time aid is driven by the assumptions of outsiders rather than the knowledge of insiders (those who understand first-hand the obstacles and opportunities within their communities), it is rendered less effective. There comes a time in the poverty-disaster-instability morass when the model of humanitarian intervention must segue from high-cost, short-term relief activities pinned to an expatriate infrastructure, to tackling chronic deficits and vulnerabilities. It is a difficult transition, and one that is predisposed to fail. Why?

It fails in part because international NGOs, UN agencies, and other purveyors of aid have differing opinions about when to make the transition. In Darfur, a decade after the most aggressive and intense period of conflict, nearly 3 million people continue to live in camps for the internally displaced, where they depend on emergency provisions – a decade of waiting to return to a life that no longer exists. While the focus of aid spending in Darfur is now moving on to early recovery rather than relief initiatives, emergency funds continue to be the norm if international govenment donors are interested at all – and most are not. This money provides food, water, shelter, health, and basic education, while young men in the camps become increasingly marginalized and disillusioned. They are easy marks for local militias, whose recruitment is aided by poverty and unemployment. With "popular" crises such as the Haiti earthquake and the 2004 tsunami, relief organizations often have more money than they can spend, while development organizations (both local and international) that do not also engage in relief operations wrestle with shoestring or non-existent budgets. Technically it would have been possible for the groups who received the lion's share of the 2004 tsunami allocations to grant some of it to smaller development organizations with a proven track record. But the world's biggest NGOs have the institutional psychology of most large multinationals: Why throw bones to the competition?

By the end of 2007 the Canadian Red Cross still had $200 million in unspent tsunami funding, more than half of the money they received from donors three years earlier. Apart from the reputational damage this causes any humanitarian organization reliant on public funding, instances such as these also provide an opening for miscreants and demagogues to popularly evict aid workers as self-interested opportunists – thereby, conveniently, also eliminating the possibility of independent witness to atrocities. In Sri Lanka in 2008, as Mahinda Rajapaksa's government was pushing deeper into Tamil-held areas and the body count began to rise, the government exploited the high-cost, low-yield post-tsunami efforts of international NGOs in Sri Lanka to justify expelling them or otherwise frustrating their efforts to reach Tamil civilians under siege. The local media ran multiple stories parroting the government's position that international NGOs were little more than career opportunists who'd failed Sri Lankans. It was not difficult for Sri Lankans to accept the government's position, because many had witnessed the wastage.

Even large organizations with a dual relief and development mandate, such as World Vision or Oxfam, are under tremendous pressure to quickly spend emergency funds on high-visibility, life-saving interventions. Moved to action by current events, donors have an expectation that their funds will be used immediately and not slowly allocated to programs in-country over the next decade. Humanitarian appeals do little to offset this by emphasizing that help is needed *today*. And yet, this is *precisely* what the aid sector needs: more longevity and less reactivity. It is not only the business of aid that needs to change, but also the expectations of those contributing to it. Otherwise, history is condemned to repeat itself.

Finally, the current aid model fails because organizations that rely predominantly on deploying foreigners from wealthy countries invariably create a distance between themselves and the communities they serve. With time and effort, this distance contracts, but not when international NGOs remain segregated from local civil society, closeted in Euro-American enclaves. Liberia taught me, ingloriously, that the aid community is an exclusive club bent on reinforcing its own stereotypes and rewarding its friends. Grants are often announced over cocktails and pre-approved during dinner parties. If you're not present, you're shut out. For local organizations and civil society leaders, the system is virtually impenetrable.

Aid is critical to the creation of more peaceful, just, and equitable societies. Its effectiveness cannot be measured by economic growth alone. It is proven effective through increased social stability, including school enrolment (especially of girls), strengthened democracy, better health outcomes, and decreased vulnerability to war, famine, disease, and natural disasters. Sometimes the changes are subtle, evident in the hope expressed in casual conversations and in the incremental dismantling of psychological barriers, such as girls previously forbidden from attending school who dream of one day becoming doctors. Success cannot always be measured in numbers or even at a national level, but may be revealed through examples of innovation and local participation that provide proof only in their possibilities.

To improve the effectiveness of aid, the humanitarian movement must recalibrate, focusing more on knowledge transference, training, and on reducing the obstacles to local engagement and participation. This can never be achieved through the creation of ever-larger field offices staffed overwhelmingly with foreigners in decision-making roles while disenfranchised communities wait for life to change. Neither can it be accomplished by consolidating aid and public goodwill into billion-dollar enterprises, or by opening the floodgates to tacky, one-off disaster safaris (more on this subject in Chapter 5). Above all, the humanitarian sector – and all who support and embrace it – must reaffirm its commitment to first do no harm.

The war in Burundi, during the mid 1990s, was like Rwanda in slow motion. I arrived in the country in 1997 to help with an investigation, undertaken by Brown University's Department of Humanitarianism and War, into the civilian impact of recently imposed economic sanctions on the country. A year earlier, Tutsi President Pierre Buyoya had seized power in a military coup. More than 100,000 people were killed, with widespread atrocities committed against both Hutu and Tutsi civilians. In the evenings, I would often sit on the balcony of a local restaurant in Bujumbura overlooking Lake Tanganyika, reviewing my notes. At the time, on the other side of the lake, Laurent Kabila had just begun his bloody assault towards the Zairean capital of Kinshasa as Hutu militias in eastern Congo continued their rampage. Desperate Congolese civilians, struggling to escape the murderous front, constructed rafts with logs and twine upon which they loaded themselves and their small children, then pushed into the deep waters. Very few could swim, and many of the rafts capsized or disintegrated long before they reached their equally hellish destination. The suffocating fear in war invites human beings to make such anguished choices.

I ventured along Lake Tanganyika's shores only once. There, between the tall grasses and sandy inlets, floated the decomposing bodies of Zairean civilians scattered among their personal possessions: clothes, children's sandals, and grass mats. The bodies were bloated, the colour of magenta; not recognizably human. It was rumoured that Buyoya's military had been given orders to shoot refugees arriving across Lake Tanganyika as soon as they were in range, on the basis that they might be returning Hutu *génocidaires*. Most of the bodies were missing limbs or heads, crudely severed by the area's voracious crocodiles.

As part of the assessment, I arranged to visit the northern areas of the country. The humanitarian situation in the north was dire, with a dramatic shortage of food and medical supplies.

The roads were too dangerous to travel except by armoured car.

From the back of an armoured UNHCR vehicle, with its shrunken windows and weighted frame, the road to Ngozi was a steady, undulating climb. Velvet jungles abruptly opened onto smouldering, logged fields, then folded into stepped rows of coffee plants spread out across the countryside. We passed local villagers carrying baskets of bright-red coffee berries to be sorted and dried by hand. This scene repeated itself every hour, until the number of pedestrians thinned and the jungle once again began to thicken.

As the vehicle heaved around a narrow corner, I caught my first long view of the valley. The rest I remember only in flashes. A man and a small child, no more than seven, their hands roped together. They are blindfolded. The child is in school shorts. There are two adolescent boys with Kalashnikov rifles. One walks beside the man and kicks him in the leg. He stumbles. The child falls forward. The other boy stands at the back, the butt of the gun on his hip, his hand on the trigger. He sees me watching through the window. Did he smile at me? Was he taunting me?

"Stop the car!" I shout. "Stop the car!" The driver slows but does not stop. He is nervous. I pull at the door handle. "Damn it. I said stop the car! Please. They're going to kill them!" I am shrieking. "He's a little boy. Please. Stop the fucking car!"

The vehicle does not stop. My driver is yelling in French, his hands gripping the wheel, his foot firmly on the accelerator. "Stop? To do what? What will you do? Tell me. *Qu'est-ce que vous allez faire?*"

The man and the boy are on their knees. The Kalashnikovs are pointed at their backs.

"Please." I am begging now. "We have to do something."

"If you want to die, that is your choice," he says, with finality. "But you do not decide when it is my time. Do you understand? If I stop this car, they will kill us all." We keep moving forward, faster now.

I buried my face in my hands and cried. I did not see what happened.

I live not knowing whether I could have done more that day in Burundi. But only fools rush in believing they have the answers, not realizing how quickly they become part of the problem.

CHAPTER 5

PACK YOUR BAGS,
WE'RE GOING ON A GUILT TRIP

*It is much more easy to have sympathy with suffering
than it is to have sympathy with thought.*
OSCAR WILDE

"Tell me why you want to speak to the women," demanded the village Chairman as he swatted at flies.

Mariam, a Somali midwife in her fifties, was indomitable. "We are here to talk to the women about their health, about women's problems," she said, adjusting her orange abaya but never showing our hosts the deference they appeared to be expecting. "We want to know how women are coping in these difficult times."

Mariam had taught nursing at Mogadishu University, until warring factions turned the city into a murderous wasteland. After fleeing with her adult children to Baidoa, she was hired by UNICEF to lead several women's health initiatives, including a pilot program to curb the horrific practice of female genital mutilation, which she had openly condemned in her classrooms. It was a defiant, progressive stance at a time when the prevailing view was that this cruel amputation made young girls "cleaner."

The Chairman was unmoved by her answer and would not be cut short by a woman. "We men, too, have problems," he responded, as the elders nodded with approval. He snapped his fingers at the air, and women poured hot, scarlet Shah Hawaash tea into a pair of shot glasses, which were passed around the group. Cardamom, cinnamon, and cloves masked the smell of cooking fires and sweat.

The men began a conversation that drifted into herds lost to drought, blocked trade routes, and a barter system that no longer provided for the basic necessities of life. An elder spoke of the anguish of losing all the young, agile men to war, and of having little choice but to return to the back-breaking work of tilling the fields. Mariam was patient and precise, responding sympathetically while remaining persistent with her request. I was frustrated and overheated, and wondered how much longer this could possibly take. I was also beginning to realize I'd accepted one ceremonial bush tea too many, and the only tree in sight was the one ineptly shading our conversation.

The elders wondered when the rains would come, and how many more sons would be sacrificed to the fighting engulfing their remote village. "What can we do?" they asked. They compared notes on rheumatism, fatigue, and swollen ankles. The discussion continued in this vein for no less than an eternity. It would soon be dusk, at which point it would be too risky to make the 100-kilometre drive back to Baidoa. Even Mariam started to show her frustration. "We are not leaving," she finally announced, "until we speak to the women."

The thought of a UN vehicle and its occupants attracting attention overnight did not appeal to the elders, and so the women were finally convened. They dutifully gathered in a one-room, thatched hut, filling the space with bright colours and conversation. Inside, their headscarves fell to their shoulders. Tea was again offered.

Mariam began, her mood relaxed and satisfied. "*Salaam alaikum.* I am here to talk to you about something very important." The women, about forty of them ranging from sixteen to seventy, moved closer. Mariam asked how many could read. None put up her hand. She reached into her woven satchel, pulled out a photocopied book of illustrations, and opened it to the first page. "This is how we are born as girls." She showed the women pencil drawings of normal female anatomy. The younger women giggled. One covered her mouth. A few older women made hissing sounds at the men, who had started to convene outside the entrance to the hut.

Mariam carefully turned the page. "This is what happens during infibulation." The pictures were graphic, but not gratuitous. There was an illustration of a young girl on a mat, her legs spread open, a straight razor cutting away her labia. A pool of dark blood was shown beneath her buttocks. The illustrated girl appeared grief-stricken and confused.

As the discussion ensued, the men became emboldened, surrounding the hut and monitoring the conversation through gaps in its walls of mud and dung. They whispered to one another, like teenage boys peeping into the girls' locker room. The women shifted uncomfortably.

Mariam continued, unfazed by the attention she was generating. "This is what happens during childbirth, when a woman is the same as Allah made her." She passed around a drawing of a woman in labour, with the infant's head crowning. Then she pointed to the final pictures in the series: a woman in obstructed labour, and another hemorrhaging while her baby lay dead beside her. "And this is what happens when a woman has been cut as a girl, against the will of Allah."

In Somalia, female genital mutilation is forced onto girls as young as four and involves the complete removal of the clitoris and labia. During childbirth, the thick vaginal scarring often forces the infant out through the woman's rectum, which, if she survives the subsequent hemorrhage and infection, results in fecal incontinence and social isolation. Female genital mutilation, often wrongly characterized as "circumcision," is not a cultural or religiously sanctioned practice.

The men became raucous. Those with a clear view of the proceedings shouted back to the other men in the crowd, which was expanding. Mariam asked the women whether they had any questions. The men's presence was clearly intimidating to the women, who no longer maintained eye contact with Mariam.

The eldest woman in the group was a qaat-chewing traditional birth attendant with deeply wrinkled skin and a stained, solitary tooth. Resolute, she moved towards the entrance of the hut and shouted something to the loitering men. Inside, the women exploded with laughter and applause, cheering and whistling at her. Through the holes in the walls, the men could be seen sprinting away from the hut – literally falling over one another – kicking up sand as they made their retreat.

Mariam smiled brightly and dutifully explained to me what had happened. "That old woman, she just yelled out, 'Hey, all you men! We are in here talking about vaginas. If you want to come in here and talk about vaginas, you are most welcome. Otherwise, get lost!'"

"Even in my country," I said to the women, as Mariam translated, "whenever women start talking about vaginas, suddenly all the men disappear." This sparked another round of uproarious laughter.

TO BE PRESENT for these conversations — these moments of education, revelation, and sisterhood — is to confront our assumptions. The entire humanitarian movement and the cacophony of NGOs it has spawned are, to melancholic effect, anchored to the myth of a poor, nebulous "Other" (in deference to Ryszard Kapuscinski): *Hurry, we must save them.* This is what moves us to give, and it is the lens through which we often see people living in developing nations — particularly, though by no means exclusively, on the African continent. This has not changed substantively over the past half century, despite immigration, the rise of multiculturalism, and globalization. "You're going to an Ethiopian restaurant?" goes the joke. "What do they serve, an empty plate?"

Among western nations, the quest to cast those living with war and abject poverty as helpless creates illusions that are both regressive and harmful. We are inundated with images of the poor, starving African child. Her face appears on our television screens, her eyes searching as Anne Murray croons in the background, "*I cried a tear . . .*" This is followed by several gratuitous slow-motion montages of squalor and morbid desperation, before, "*You needed me.*" The ads are excruciating to watch and yet, in terms of generating donations for organizations that produce them, highly effective. They work precisely because they manipulate ignorance and guilt. The children are never too old (under ten) to cause us to question their innocence, and therefore their worthiness, and donors can choose who among the forlorn they want to "sponsor," based on such criteria as geography, age, and gender. Sponsors receive photographs and details of their child, as if she were a Cabbage Patch Doll. Or a Pound Puppy. *There now, we saved you.*

Many organizations relying on child sponsorship openly acknowledge that the money doesn't actually go to that *specific* child – it is invested in community-based development. The letters, and photos, and details that donors receive merely represent the *kind* of children who benefit from such support. But donors cling to the notion that this is their "foster child," and charities benefiting from sponsorship programs do little to dispel this. Why else would the appeals to "support your child" continue into late adolescence, alongside updated personal "letters"? *Caveat donor*, perhaps?

Perhaps, but the broader impact of this type of mass marketing (also known as "poverty porn") must not be ignored, because it perpetuates racial stereotypes and ultimately marginalizes the very communities such programs are intended to serve. It does this by portraying people living with war and poverty as passive recipients of charity who are perpetually waiting for outsiders to change the circumstances of their lives. These campaigns reduce ubiquitous inequalities to simple messages designed to make us believe that these don't matter as much as one child whose future is in *our* hands. These are the vestiges of neo-colonialism, cloaked in altruism. And this is precisely why these appeals are highly effective. Efforts to curb such practices by creating volunteer standards that would restrict charities from staging the circumstances of children's lives, or using images that could potentially stereotype them, have been proposed by both UNICEF and the Irish Association of Non-Governmental Organizations (DOCHAS). These have failed to gain support among most organizations reliant on sponsorship fundraising models.

What does it mean, then, to *do good*? This is a complex question, because the simple act of helping has its own rewards. It provides meaning and context to our lives, offers a respite from materialism, and fosters a sense of purpose and belonging. To give is a privilege. Andrew Carnegie, Bill and Melinda Gates, John and Catherine MacArthur, Warren Buffett, Richard Branson, George Soros, and Onsi Sawiris are among those who have built legacies through philanthropy.* Their charitable giving brought additional influence and acclaim, and in many instances has shaped development priorities and public policy. Giving, in ways either large or small, therefore comes with its own set of responsibilities. Charity can unwittingly create dependency and may be inappropriate or even humiliating. When humanitarian action is couched in paternalistic language and deeds — when it is framed as *saving the meek* — there is the stigma of indignity attached to it. The best, most successful humanitarian programs are respectful and consultative, and are driven by the priorities of local stakeholders. But this is not what we typically reward with our charitable giving on this side of the world. Instead, the injustices endured by the impoverished and the war-ravaged become the backdrop to our quest for personal or emotional fulfillment, and not the other way around.

There are some alarming trends in how we engage in aid and development, and how we give. I've already talked about the danger that unprofessional groups present to humanitarian operations, as well as the need for greater balance between short-term relief operations (tied to external expertise) versus longer-term, sustainable development programming. But there are other examples of the ways in which we deliberately undermine and compromise the very people we claim to be "helping."

One example is the exploding industry of volunteer tourism. There are various iterations of the concept, but they typically

---

* Purposefully excluded from this list is Henry Ford, whose philanthropic legacy can never excuse his perfervid anti-Semitism.

involve a developing country and a packaged experience of meals, accommodations, tourist attractions, and an activity such as building a classroom, digging a well, or volunteering at an orphanage. At about $5,000 to $12,000 per person, these "voluntours" promise a rewarding vacation experience in which participants briefly forge emotional attachments to local communities and leave with greater self-awareness after being schooled in "development." The media have keenly profiled such excursions, which *Time* magazine called "getting in touch with your inner Angelina Jolie." Widely popular with high school, church, college groups, and alumni associations, these mass-marketed stints have displaced outback canoe trips as the character-building adventures of a lifetime.

So, what's wrong with voluntourism? Isn't it an important way of exposing people from the North to the challenges of the South, educating them about development, and providing the kind of direct linkages that will transform them into global citizens? How else will young people gain this kind of experience when established NGOs routinely turn down offers for overseas volunteers? And what about all the money these trips raise for local initiatives?

In the first instance, these short-term, everyone-is-welcome experiences are rarely offered or administered by many of the world's leading international aid agencies, and for good reason: they make a spectacle out of poverty and expose overseas communities – especially children – to exploitation and abuse. Voluntour programs are largely administered by for-profit entities whose primary accountability is to their paying clients (who require clean water, good food, comfortable accommodations, assurances of security, and stimulating tasks), not the "recipients" overseas. A village in rural Kenya may urgently need an old pit latrine filled in, or dead cattle hauled from the drinking water supply, but good luck pitching either as the feel-good vacation of a lifetime.

Applicants to reputable international volunteer organizations like Canadian Crossroads International, Engineers Without Borders (EWB), and Voluntary Service Overseas (VSO) are required to undergo a rigorous screening process and to demonstrate relevant knowledge. Voluntour programs, however, are typically open to anyone willing to foot the bill. VSO has openly criticized the growing voluntourism industry, calling it "outdated and colonial." In some cases, local conditions are reputed to be kept deliberately squalid so that visitors will be convinced of the authenticity and need (and thus be likely to reach into their pockets a few more times before departing). It is an industry that capitalizes on good intentions while relying on a lack of awareness about what constitutes meaningful development.

In many ways, the charitable sector has only itself to blame, for trying to appease donors by commodifying complex social and economic issues. Participants in voluntour vacations often believe that their labour is a more transparent and direct way of giving than simply writing a cheque and trusting that an experienced, well-established organization will use it responsibly. But there's an arrogance embedded in the assumption that by dint of being born on this side of the world, our presence and unskilled labour are of intrinsic value to those who don't share our advantages.

Reputable international aid agencies are wary of accepting untrained, inexperienced volunteers for overseas placements not just because of the associated costs and risks, but also because they have a moral and professional duty to the communities they serve. A revolving door of unskilled workers on the ground in two-week increments is more of a burden than a benefit to any community. The bonds that are formed and then routinely broken with children, especially orphaned children, during such sojourns can have a devastating impact on their emotional and psychological health. Repeated short-term attachments can leave young children with feelings of abandonment that impede their social development. Visitors to these programs often come away with a sense of how friendly and happy the children were, and it is common to see photos and promotional videos on voluntour websites of foreigners ferrying affectionate children about on their shoulders and backs. But what creates an extraordinary experience for the visitors – hyper-friendly preschoolers who make them feel immediately wanted – is a symptom of the children's repeated psychological trauma. It is normal for young children to be cautious, even mistrustful of strangers. That children in these programs are so emotionally indiscriminate should be heeded as a warning that voluntour programs are failing children, rather than lauded as evidence of how much the foreigners were appreciated. Voluntour participants typically refer to the "deep bonds" they formed with children and how meaningful the experience was for them, without realizing that therein lies the problem.

I recognize the value of exposing young professionals to humanitarian work and I am a product of such opportunities. I would not have chosen the path I've been on since graduating from medical school had I not been presented with a volunteer position with UNICEF. But there are some important distinctions. I had already completed my medical degree and was almost finished a relevant master's degree in Public Health in Developing Countries. I was not responsible for the direct delivery of services, and I was working in a supporting role *for* national staff, not the other way around. And at no point was I invited to take pictures with orphans in the morning and giraffes in the afternoon.

Ethical, responsible development programs serve the needs

of communities first, not the yearnings of students in their gap years. With every school that is built by well-meaning western volunteers in impoverished villages in Africa, there is one less opportunity to provide employment and skills training to young people living in those communities, who are also desperately seeking such experiences. Agencies organizing these projects argue that they create a lasting connection for participants, and forever change the way they view development. But that's precisely the problem: *we* are the ones deriving the greatest educational and social benefit. Schools are also not built through construction labour alone. To be effective in promoting education and creating genuine opportunities for vulnerable children, local teachers must be trained to national curricular standards, salaries must be paid (preferably by local government), and the issue of school fees, an ongoing obstacle for poor children globally, must be addressed. And there must be a continued investment in community outreach to sustain girls' enrollment, which is critical to breaking the cycle of poverty and despair. Voluntour programs, by promiscuous design, shortchange local communities by circumventing these broader challenges.

It's understandable that major donors want to see the impact of their contributions. A non-intrusive visit from representatives of a foundation or active donors, for example, might lead to a deeper understanding of the work, and ultimately more funding. But there's a discernible difference between supporting the work and *taking it over*.

"Travel," wrote Mark Twain, "is fatal to prejudice, bigotry and narrow-mindedness." Travellers looking to make a difference need not waste their money on busy-work philanthropy. Their dollars would be better spent supporting local trades by buying handmade crafts in markets, choosing fair-trade products, or by making a donation to a reputable development organization. And there is a wide range of eco-vacation programs that offer ethical tourism experiences for the socially conscious without stripping local communities of labour income or placing their children in vulnerable situations.

Students with an aptitude for human rights concerns and global issues can participate in a number of campaigns and educational events offered by a range of organizations, from Amnesty International and Global Witness, to Model United Nations Assemblies and EWB youth conferences. Many NGOs also offer non-field volunteer positions and student employment programs. These may lack the glamour of overseas expeditions, but they are an excellent introduction to the work of the organizations and to the lessons of development. Humanitarian organizations value such employment credentials far more than an obvious voluntour safari, which, among veteran aid workers, packs all the résumé punch of a scarlet letter.

The mainstreaming of NGOs, and humanitarian aid more generally, has fostered an exuberant generation of extracurricular aid workers who want to roll up their sleeves and be at the centre of the action. This commitment is commendable, as is the desire to volunteer overseas. But the best of intentions do not guarantee the best outcomes.

The current concept of foreign aid – now more formally called *official* or *overseas* development assistance (ODA) – to the "Third World" dates back to 1969 (note: "Third World" is an offensive characterization that needs to be tossed from our lexicon*). A

---

* I admit "developing countries" may not be much of an improvement, but at least it is no longer being treated like a horse race.

commission chaired by former Canadian Prime Minister Lester B. Pearson examined the World Bank's past record of development aid, and mapped out a plan for the future. One of the commission's significant recommendations was that wealthy nations commit a minimum of 0.7 percent of their Gross National Product, a measure of a country's overall wealth, to aid in developing nations. As many former colonies moved towards self-governance (often in the hands of western puppets), they remained dangerously disadvantaged after more than a century of economic exploitation. To that end, while ODA is traditionally viewed as a magnanimous transfer of wealth from rich countries to poorer ones, it is more accurately a form of voluntary restitution for a debt of historic injustice that may be impossible to repay.

More than forty years later, most nations are a long way from meeting the 0.7 percent target and, in North America at least, despite several high-profile campaigns there has been very little political movement towards this goal. In 2016, during the largest famine and refugee crisis since World War II, only six countries met United Nations' ODA targets as a percentage of their gross national income (GNI): The United Arab Emirates (1.12 percent); Norway (1.14 percent); Luxembourg (1.004 percent); Sweden (0.937 percent); Turkey (0.79 percent), and Denmark (0.753 percent). Two of the world's major arms exporters, the United Kingdom and Germany, came close (just shy of 0.7 percent), while aid funding levels in Canada, Australia, France, and the United States dropped to less than 0.3 percent. In sheer dollar terms, the United States is still the largest contributor at $36.4 billion, but does not look nearly as good when its contributions are measured as a percentage of national wealth, coming in at 0.18 percent in 2016 – or twenty-sixth in the world, despite its P5 member status at the United Nations. Canada is also an ODA laggard, with levels that have dropped in recent years from an already abysmal 0.3 to 0.26 percent – under a Liberal government that declared itself to be "back" on the world stage. Both Canada and the United States are quick to cut ODA contributions on flimsy excuses that range from fiscal "belt tightening" to thinly veiled nationalism. ("We have to look after our own first.") Joseph Nye, Jr., Harvard professor and former assistant secretary of defence, has called the cuts "an easy vote, but a cheap shot" asserting that it ultimately erodes American influence on global affairs. One of President Trump's first presidential promises was to cut American ODA by 30 percent while increasing the military budget.

The goal of achieving 0.7 percent has been criticized as being both arbitrary and meaningless. Shouldn't the priority be to make aid better, eliminating the waste and corruption, before spending more on it? Especially when those aid funds are going to governments of unstable countries, which are more inclined to use them to prop up their militaries and their lifestyles than to benefit their citizens? The answer to misspent aid, however, is not to cut it back. That would have only a modest impact on oppressive and corrupt regimes, which, like that of former Zimbabwean president Robert Mugabe who ruled for thirty years, are deftly resilient to any attempt at economic strangulation. On the contrary, aid spending through local and international NGOs is even more necessary in such circumstances, to protect against the human rights abuses and civilian suffering that accompany tyranny by promoting community resilience and strengthening civil society. And yet we spend remarkably less on ODA, particularly in relation to military spending, than we ought to, given its critical role in promoting stability and tackling underlying inequities.

Improving aid's effectiveness and reaching ODA targets are tandem steps. The success of aid programs is not only a function of how aid is being spent, but also a function of *how much* there is to spend. A reliable flow of ODA allows aid groups to deliver their programs consistently, over sustained periods. I've seen many outstanding aid programs wasted because funding levels were cut, or political priorities shifted. It takes years for aid to really work; quick results are rarely lasting ones. From a development perspective, for example, Afghanistan has not been a failure. Looking beyond the malignant profiteering and systemic corruption of the Afghan government for a moment, standards of health, education, and development have improved in many quarters of Afghanistan because of ODA. Local and international NGOs have been critical to this process. It will take another decade of substantive ODA support for Afghan civilians, especially women and girls, to have confidence in the future. This is where NGOs play an important role. That ODA to Afghanistan is increasingly being consolidated (in the form of bilateral assistance to the local government) is yet another example of political irrationality when it comes to aid expenditures. In theory, of course, it makes absolute sense to diminish the role of local and international aid agencies in Afghanistan and to empower the government to deliver social services. But in an accountability vacuum, and in the face of an erratic leadership, this transition ought to proceed incrementally and cautiously. And certainly not at the expense of Afghan civil society groups, who in many ways are more responsive and transparent (and enjoy greater local legitimacy) than the most elected Afghan officials. Aid, in and of itself, cannot overcome broader structural deficits (corruption, despotism, militarism, fanaticism) that fuel fragile states; however, when carefully managed and timed, it can help erode them.

Where ODA levels have stagnated, private philanthropy appears to be filling at least part of the void through major global initiatives targeting AIDS, malaria, and other infectious diseases. Warren Buffett and Bill Gates have challenged America's billionaires to commit half of their wealth to charity, and have demonstrated a strong commitment to international causes. Private philanthropy has the advantage of being more versatile and responsive than government funding. But it is not a substitute for sound ODA policy, particularly because it can be so easily subverted by ideology or special interests. Philanthropy may be critical to the delivery of humanitarian programs around the world, but should not be relied upon to compensate for ODA contributions that are woefully inadequate.

An Iraqi friend of mine, Aquila al-Hashimi, was a senior bureaucrat in the Oil for Food Programme* at the Iraqi Foreign Ministry. She was from a prominent, educated Shia family and held a doctorate in French literature from the Sorbonne. Aquila was outspoken, elegantly refined, and critical of Iraq's dictatorship, not in what she said (like most of Iraq's democratic proponents, she would have been tortured and executed for speaking out) but in what was notably absent from our conversations. Over the course of nearly a decade, I never once heard Aquila profess her support for Saddam or any other member of the Ba'ath Party, which was standard operating procedure for bureaucrats forever looking over their shoulders. She was also known for taking risks to push

---

* The United Nations' Oil for Food Programme was intended to allow Iraq, under the strict control of the United Nations, to sell oil on the world market in order to obtain aid, such as food and medicine, while blocking the country from boosting its military capabilities.

through visas for aid workers in Iraq, including my own on several occasions, by personally approving the applications. In a political climate where most civil servants survived by playing Duck and Cover with every decision, Aquila was forthright and sincere.

Long before the Oil for Food Programme's mismanagement and embezzlement became a media story, Aquila could provide an inventory of ongoing transgressions that were as shameful as they were shocking. There was little, however, she could do about it. Allegations against foreign officials or United Nations agencies involved with the program could be skirted by simply dismissing them as Iraqi propaganda, or by fingering Hussein's kleptocracy. It was, in that sense, an easy crime: cash holdings transferred in pinball-like fashion between multiple bank accounts; a loose system for approving compensation claims and suppliers; and plausible deniability. Created in 1995, the Oil for Food Programme was designed to appease growing international concern about the exploding death toll among Iraqi civilians attributed to the blanket economic sanctions in place since Iraq's invasion of Kuwait in 1990 – sanctions that were more punitive than any used against a population either before or since. But under the deal, which totalled over $60 billion, roughly 65 percent was actually applied to aid. The rest was spent on reimbursements to those still out of pocket for the 1991 Gulf War or who were otherwise seeking damages from Saddam, including (appropriately) war reparations to Kuwait.

I recall one particular conversation with Aquila in 2001. As I sat in her Baghdad office in the Foreign Ministry – a bland, modernist 1960s building with nicotine-stained walls and rotting plaster – she launched into a litany of complaints about abuses in the Oil for Food Programme. She threw out numbers and details, even lists of medications awaiting procurement, in alphabetical order, from memory. I knew then that she wasn't merely doing her job: she was keeping score. Aquila had once studied law, and spoke with prosecutorial precision. All United Nations salaries and costs that were billed to the Oil for Food Programme, from consultants to vehicles, crossed her desk. Just that month, she had received a claim for 193 UN "electricity consultants" at an average monthly salary of $15,000 each, while the electrical grid never worked for more than a few hours at a time. Iraqi engineers, working on the same project, were paid $500 a month. By the time the program was axed in 2003, administrative costs alone billed to Oil for Food by the United Nations totalled $1.1 billion.

Aquila was furious with UNICEF, which wanted to import $10 million in high-protein biscuits she knew to be culturally unfamiliar and inappropriate. "You must re-educate your mothers," a UNICEF official arrogantly told her when she proposed alternatives. A far simpler solution would have been to lower prices by removing all restrictions on food imports, which hurt civilians far more than they hurt Saddam's regime. But that would have meant acknowledging that the sanctions as designed were flawed policy, which, if you'll forgive the obvious pun, there was little appetite for. Worst of all, she complained, $13 billion in humanitarian aid contracts was being held up in an account at the Banque Nationale de Paris over absurd clerical issues: demands for more information on common antibiotics, trivial spelling and translation errors, and the like.

Eventually, an eighteen-month UN-sanctioned investigation into the program revealed high-level corruption, including kick-backs and illegal surcharges, involving United Nations officials and other foreigners party to the process – allegations that would also embroil former secretary general Kofi Annan's son, Kojo Annan, who was a key contractor under the Oil for Food Programme. Of course, Aquila had known all of this for years. She could have easily testified against all sides to the flagrant abuses that epitomized the Oil for Food Programme and brought enormous hardship to Iraqi civilians. She would never have the chance.

"It's a question of money and business," she said to me that day, as she handed me the swollen file of medication requests that had been returned to her with approval delays. "It is not about principles, this matter of Iraq. A lot of people are benefiting from this matter of business."

While I would never discourage anyone from giving to an international cause, I would caution those genuinely motivated to help to pay close attention to what's actually needed. One of the ways that private interests can overshadow sound decision making when it comes to aid is in the shipping of products to those deemed "less fortunate" beyond our borders. I've been on the awkward end of countless phone calls and emails over the years from people inquiring about donating questionable goods, from outdated used textbooks (in English, no less, to countries where it is at best a third language), to prefab experimental temporary housing in hurricane zones, to thousands of pairs of plastic gardening sandals.* I was once contacted by a journalist seeking my opinion on a charitable venture she'd uncovered in which classrooms of children in some Catholic primary schools were being asked to hand over a portion of their Hallowe'en candy to be distributed by missionaries to "The Starving Children of Africa." She'd called

---

* Perhaps the most unusual request ever to cross my desk was from a manufacturer looking to donate his surplus of left-foot shoes, believing this would benefit amputees (right-foot amputees, to be precise) in Africa.

knowing that I would be openly critical of such a program, and I did not disappoint. Because that's exactly what children struggling with poverty and malnutrition need: melted Smarties. The urge to help is commendable, but it is never enough simply to mean well. Countries struggling to recover from war or natural disaster cannot become a dumping ground for our good intentions.

Passing surplus product along to charities has become a popular industry in North America, where tax regulations allow corporations to receive a charitable receipt for the retail value of donated goods. This is much more advantageous to corporations than selling the same product for less than the cost of manufacturing, plus they get to flaunt their status as good global citizens. Even if the product was manufactured in a sweatshop in China for significantly less than minimum wage, it can be repackaged as "corporate social responsibility" and shipped by someone else to a place where it won't affect the company's bottom line. The shipment may languish in foreign customs for months, which is, along with the payment of "incentives" to ensure their expeditious release, routine. Once distributed, some recipients will try to make the best of the handouts, others will resell their share, and local trades and vendors will have a hard time feeding their families for a few months. The loss of hundreds of thousands of textile jobs in Africa has been attributed to the trade of used clothing – largely from wealthy nations. Reputable and experienced NGOs procure most of their supplies locally to boost industry, reduce shipping costs, and ensure quality control. When it comes to humanitarian assistance, donated hard goods are rarely more than easy compassion or a cheap excuse to profit from charity.[*]

---

[*] The only exception is large volumes of donated medicines and medical supplies appropriate to the context.

At the same time, corporations are playing a more conspicuous role in the charitable sector, and many of the organizations reaping the benefits are those that comfort rather than confront corporate interests. This is dangerous for two reasons. First, it diminishes the role of NGOs as incubators of social movements designed to protect disenfranchised groups and gives corporations unprecedented control over their historic critics, eroding public accountability. And second, it can place corporate interests squarely ahead of local needs, as aid agencies contort to meet the peculiar demands of MBAs schooled in top-line equations: how many, how much, and how quickly? They emphasize high-visibility, low-cost-per-capita projects that pander to, rather than challenge, public sensibilities. In the process, less-accessible human rights and development concerns – such as war, rape, and impunity – are sidelined in favour of "brand aligned" initiatives that can be easily distilled onto the back of a box of Cheerios.

There are many companies, some of which I've had the privilege of partnering with over the years, with genuine philanthropic interests. They unconditionally support meaningful programs, and ask only how they can help, not what's in it for them. But they are the exceptions. Other corporations get directly involved in aid and development projects simply so they can promote themselves as good corporate citizens while masking more sinister violations of social, environmental, and labour standards. Corporate culture is also becoming a key influencer in reshaping the management of NGOs, with many charities retooling their organizational structures to position themselves as business-friendly. The pressure to secure corporate funds, as government donors move to cost-share on projects (positioned as a "value added" requirement on grants) and the competition for public funding intensifies, is immense. Among NGO leaders themselves,

I've noted with consternation a growing conservatism and corporate ruthlessness that risks overshadowing humanitarian principles and a rigorous knowledge of development. It matters less whether organizations are fulfilling their mandate in a responsible, evidence-based fashion and more that they can pitch a good sound bite with numbers to back it up.

Governments too are blithely parroting the rhetoric of aid "effectiveness," consolidating resources around specific geographic and thematic areas, and favouring large organizations and United Nations appeals rather than individual grants. This kind of aid consolidation is felt to be less administratively onerous, especially for government bureaucracies tasked with managing aid programs. For example, it is increasingly common for government aid donors to contribute to United Nations humanitarian pooled funds for programs in war-torn environments, rather than to deal with multiple proposals from organizations directly. The UN is then tasked with deciding which programs are worth supporting, and government donors, such as the Canadian International Development Agency (CIDA) or the U.S. Agency for International Development (USAID), are not burdened with the responsibility of monitoring or auditing multiple grants. On the surface, this appears to be a rational approach. In reality, however, United Nations agencies take a hefty administrative cut before redistributing the funds to international "implementing partners" (NGOs), who also have administrative costs that must be covered. The accountability requirement no longer rests with the government granting agency (thus circumventing the need for detailed reporting to taxpayers) but with an intermediary. Each time the aid ball bounces from one agency to another, the ODA dollars become harder to follow and the administrative costs grow. For every dollar given directly to an agency implementing an aid project, the normal administrative cost would be in the order of at least 20 percent. When aid dollars are sent to New York, then to a head office in the field, then to an implementing partner (with its own international headquarters, which must be supported for the agency to remain solvent), then to a project in the Haitian countryside, they quickly turn into pennies. Rigorous effectiveness measurements also skew aid away from high-need groups and towards those more likely to produce maximum results within the imposed timelines. The unintended result is a diminished number of opportunities overall to reduce global conflict and poverty.

NGOs don't have to be big to work. Project Ploughshares, for example, has been an uncompromising and commanding voice on nuclear disarmament and arms control for thirty-five years, and rightly measures success in terms of policy impact. The organization assesses its progress in relation to its overall goal of disarmament, rather than to an arbitrary cost-per-capita metric. But these kinds of organizations are becoming the exception, in no small part because they do not cede to political interests, nor are they conveniently positioned for a Point of Purchase donation at Walmart (especially not, given Walmart's record of firearms sales). The opposing view is that small and medium-sized organizations unable to sustain themselves without government funding should simply be allowed to collapse, and that the world will be no worse for it. And if agencies are not able to establish their added value and expertise, it's hard to justify keeping them afloat. But more often, decisions surrounding who receives aid funding, and for what ends, are based on administrative convenience, political ideology, and a bigger-is-better dogma that deserves greater scrutiny. Rather than enhancing efficiencies, such approaches are stifling innovation by creating ever-larger aid monopolies.

The humanitarian sector is now dominated by two extremes: a virtual fiefdom of large aid organizations at one end of the spectrum, and an abundance of novelty start-ups at the other end led by students, celebrities, and other assorted individuals with little relevant training, development knowledge, or experience.* The space between is rapidly evaporating.

The primary objective of aid should be to alleviate human suffering, tackle underlying inequities, and protect the vulnerable while reducing dependence. For aid to be truly effective, the providers must conduct comprehensive and ongoing assessments of gaps and opportunities at the field level. They must respect and engage local partners and communities, and be able to address the broader structural challenges, rather than simply offer a series of "one-offs." And they must be accountable directly to donors while remaining independent of corporate and political ideology and interference. It often takes a generation to see the effects of well-managed aid. And it often takes no less than a generation of ongoing commitment and partnership to arrive there.

The day before I was to leave Iraq in the late spring of 2003, I set off to find Aquila. An NBC news producer who had recently interviewed her told me that Aquila was at her home in one of Baghdad's more established neighbourhoods. Her phones were apparently

---

* Madonna's plans to build a girls' school in Malawi ended abruptly in early 2011 when it was uncovered that the project had wasted nearly $4 million before it had even broken ground, after displacing villagers from their ancestral land. Oprah Winfrey's forays into girls' education also ended in disappointment, when a dormitory matron at a school she'd built in South Africa was charged with abusing students.

down and she rarely ventured out. With the arrival of U.S. troops, reports had begun to surface of confused and frightened Iraqis coming under fire in front of military checkpoints, and of women being inappropriately frisked and harassed during routine searches. The producer could not recall Aquila's exact address but was able to draw a vague map of her location, spanning approximately eight city blocks. In any North American city of over 6 million people, a foreigner with a limited grasp of the language showing up in a residential area with nothing more than a name would likely not get very far. But in Baghdad, families often live in close proximity for generations, which, combined with a fastidious need to know your extended neighbours for reasons of self-preservation, made it a safe bet that her home would not take long to locate.

The drive over was, in the manner that had become routine, excruciating. I counted twenty checkpoints. Every time, the vehicle was stopped. Every time, the driver was made to get out of the car so the trunk, glove compartment, and underside of the seats could be searched. Every time, we were asked to explain our "purpose of business." Streets ended abruptly in concrete barricades or were blocked with tanks – the turret, on at least one occasion, pointed directly at us. My cab driver came to such frequent and sudden halts that I expected my throat to eventually land somewhere on the dash. (As someone who suffers from inconvenient bouts of car sickness, I can safely claim to have vomited at the side of the road in no fewer than forty-two countries.) "*Yalla, yalla,*" I kept pleading. Let's go, let's go. But he just shook his head and made soft downward gestures with his hands, reminding me to be patient.

It was a hot day and the cab's air conditioning, as the driver explained, had surrendered sometime around the 1991 Gulf War. Replacement parts could not be imported under the sanctions, and he'd simply made a habit of dipping his keffiyeh in water and then wrapping it around his head. From the overwhelming smell of diesel, the exhaust appeared to be discharging directly into the back seat – an unpleasantness made even worse by opening the window and breathing in the traffic vapours. By the time the driver lit his first cigarette I was truly convinced I'd run out of "least worst" options and rested my head firmly between my knees.

I recognize that the sacred illusion of the doctor-humanitarian is one that conjures up images of fearless, resilient, and sturdy characters – not bookish, asthmatic, and self-pitying ones. None are more surprised by what I ended up doing, professionally, than those who knew me in high school. I did, though, spend two very long weeks once with a pair of duelling Belgian MSF doctors in the port of Harper, Liberia, whose daily meal consisted of tuna (which they ate directly from the tin) and Club Beer, and who gave credence to the stereotype. Recovering from malaria, they would attempt to upstage each other nightly with their war stories as I withdrew to my bedroom with Vikram Seth's *A Suitable Boy* and a kerosene lamp. So the myth is not shattered entirely, I hope.

The streets of Aquila's neighbourhood were desolate, and I should not have been surprised. Lined with generous, multi-family gated compounds, it was a reasonably wealthy enclave by Baghdad's standards.* Iraqi families with the financial means to escape had moved out in the weeks leading up to the war – either to the more secure Kurdish north of the country, or to join family in other Arab states – and had no plans to return.

---

* Though larger than those in most middle-class neighbourhoods, the homes on Aquila's street still lacked running water and electricity.

We managed to find a group of boys playing soccer with a crumpled pop can. I got out of the car and asked in my broken Arabic if they knew where Aquila al-Hashimi lived. I passed my rudimentary map around. The boys discussed it at length, and a few appeared to disagree with the conclusion, but one hopped in the front of the cab anyway and began directing us. A few minutes later we pulled up to a two-storey cinder-block home, its windows crisscrossed with duct tape to prevent glass from shattering during aerial bombardment. As I stepped onto the curb, I could see Aquila watching from her living room window.

I was retrieving my bag from the back seat when she came running down her drive to greet me, all the while trying to tame her thick, coiled hair and tighten the sash on her silk bathrobe. "I am still in my dressing gown!" she shouted, warmly wrapping her arms around me and kissing the top of my head. Aquila was considerably taller than I am (in truth, most people are) and of more robust stock. Standing in front of her home, we could not have appeared more different: the queasy, elfin Canadian and the majestic, poised Iraqi.

She invited me inside and I looked forward to being able to ask her, forthrightly, about the conversations she'd been privy to at the Foreign Ministry since the last time we spoke. "There were no chemical weapons," she insisted, pouring tea as her two nieces, six and eight, pleaded for more sugar. As a Shia woman, Aquila was considered fiercely liberal and at forty-nine had never married. Her nieces were daughters to her, and, like most mothers trying to enjoy a conversation, she variously coddled and shooed them away, bargaining for one more uninterrupted minute.

"Everything crossed my desk," she continued. "*Everything*. I was present for meetings with Tariq Aziz. I listened to the conversations in the halls and around the lunch tables. I had access everywhere in the Ministry. It's impossible that this was happening and yet I heard and saw nothing. Something would have slipped. I didn't believe it then, and I don't believe it now. I was in the middle of it for more than ten years. I would have heard or seen something, *anything*. This war was based on a pack of lies." At the time, these assertions seemed radical: it was impossible to believe that the Bush administration would have waged war based on faulty or manufactured evidence of weapons of mass destruction. As she spoke, I couldn't help but wonder whether she was really as close to the information as she presumed. It would be years before she was proven right.

We passed the afternoon talking about Iraq's future and what Aquila might do next. She seemed at once peaceful and melancholic. She had avoided going to the Foreign Ministry to collect her things because she could not bear to watch as it was looted and burned: she was furious at American troops for standing down as decades of archival history were destroyed. But she was also looking forward to returning to her first love, French literature, and was considering a professorship from the University of Baghdad.

As we talked and brewed more tea on an old propane camp stove in her kitchen, the two little girls began speaking to me in French. "*Parlez-vous français?*" asked the older one, while her sister danced about chanting, "*Bonjour! Bonjour!*" I replied in French, and the two of them appeared totally confused – they'd obviously mastered the greeting, but not the response.

I asked Aquila if she'd been teaching the girls French. "Yes," she said, proudly, "I have promised them that, now that the war is over and the sanctions will end, we will go to Paris. I have been showing them the stamps in my passport from when I studied at the Sorbonne." The girls opened Aquila's passport for me. I can still vividly remember staring at her photo, taken years before, and sensing the anticipation it captured. There she was, her long hair parted in the centre, eight years of the Iran-Iraq war behind her, about to pursue her dream of reading Balzac in one of Europe's most celebrated cities.

"I feel," Aquila said as I flipped through the dog-eared pages of her passport, "as if the last thirty years have been confiscated from me. First by Saddam Hussein. Then by the Iran-Iraq war, the first Gulf War and the sanctions, and now by this most recent U.S.-led war." She then paused, as if she was searching to believe the words she was about to say. "I hope that it is over, because I am ready to live my life."

That July, despite aspiring to a quiet academic life with her family, Aquila was one of just three women appointed by the United States to Iraq's Interim Governing Council. She was an obvious choice: a progressive, educated Iraqi woman with extensive Foreign Ministry experience who understood how to broker deals with western heads of state. As a prominent Shia, she also appealed to Iraq's ethnic majority, even if her politics were secular.

On September 20, 2003, as Aquila was leaving her home for the Governing Council office, a group of assailants opened fire on her vehicle. It was early morning in Toronto when the phone startled me, and I was unable to fully grasp what I was hearing. "Sam, I'm sorry to wake you, but I thought you should know." My friend Tara Sutton, a freelance documentary filmmaker who would spend years covering the impact of the war on Iraqi civilians, was on the line from Baghdad. "Aquila's been shot. She's going to be transferred to an American military hospital. I'll try to get you a number. Sam, it sounds quite serious. I'm so sorry. I know how close you were."

The BBC ran footage from the front of Aquila's home: her bullet-punctured car, a bloody driveway, and two little girls, her nieces, standing at the side of the road sobbing. Aquila was shot several times in the abdomen. I was able to reach one of the surgeons caring for her, who explained that the bullets had shredded her pancreas. I knew then that she would not survive.

Aquila died of her injuries five days later. It was widely suspected that forces loyal to Saddam Hussein had murdered her in retribution for joining the American-backed transitional government. Others theorized that she was targeted by one of the rapidly multiplying, repugnant militia groups who condemned her for being an influential and progressive woman who walked about brazenly uncovered. No one has yet been charged in connection with her death.

Aquila, Mariam, Nadine, and the many hundreds of women and young girls I have been privileged to spend time with in war zones around the world confound every western stereotype of the hopeless, helpless victim waiting for us to rescue her. They seek justice not charity, solidarity not pity, and opportunity not handouts. Above all, they ask that we find common cause with their resilience, courage, and naked will to endure against the forces of oppression and brutality. Yes, we can get on a plane and build a school where one previously did not exist. Yes, we can ship our surplus T-shirts and flip-flops to people who have neither, and in the process enjoy a generous tax receipt. And yes, we can pick one orphaned child out of a crowd and sponsor her, or (worse) spend two weeks caring for her. But should we? For as long as we invest in outdated or self-serving models of humanitarian action, we will continue to trade in missed opportunities.

CHAPTER 6

A JUST CAUSE

During times of universal deceit,
telling the truth becomes a revolutionary act.
GEORGE ORWELL

Boarding a plane bound for Somalia sixteen years ago, I did not yet know war — its calamity, ruthlessness, and ineloquence — but was convinced of the probity of humanitarian action. To be confronted by human suffering and the poignancy of life at precisely those moments when it is mercilessly threatened is to recognize that the only indefensible response to injustice is no response at all. And yet what I failed to grasp in my rush to help was the extent to which such injustices are courted and sustained by forces often well within our control, but which we recklessly choose to ignore. Those same forces routinely implicate us in the death, mutilation, and extermination of other human beings, whose lives we degrade by casting ourselves in the role of saviours offering ever-shifting cures for their misery. When war is understood as self-destruction — as an assault against reason and the sanctity of human life — it no longer seduces us with its tales of heroism and altruism.

In the most elemental sense, we begin to solve the problem of war the moment we question it. When we challenge the rationality, for example, of manufacturing arms without end, extracting resources in unstable environments without enforceable international laws, militarism without consequence, and aid without accountability to those for whom it is intended. And while I still believe in the integrity of the NGO movement as a whole in preserving and protecting the dignity of people living with poverty and violence globally, I find no comfort in the ways in which it is evolving. Though a sure sign of advancing age is a strong sense that standards are slipping, I must convey my sense of alarm and dismay that corporate appeasement and recreational development experiences are becoming increasingly common in the NGO sector. Rather than raising the bar by increasing development literacy, an entire cottage industry of humanitarianism has been built around lowering it. There is only one way to defy this trend: expect more. And with this in mind, I'd like to humbly offer my final reflections on which initiatives I believe are worth supporting, the importance of ethical investing, the changes worth advocating for, and the criteria to apply when deciding who and what to give to.

ELIMINATING THE GENDER DIVIDE

In September 2000, world "leaders" (I've put this in quotations because not all merited this title) gathered at the United Nations in New York to adopt the United Nations Millennium Declaration, which set audacious targets to combat poverty and human misery on a global scale by 2015. These Millennium Development Goals focused on eight discrete areas: ending poverty and hunger, promoting gender equality, decreasing rates of maternal mortality, global partnerships, universal education, combating HIV/AIDS, improving child health, and environmental sustainability. Of course, over the ensuing years many things would thwart such social progress: September 11 and a refocusing of foreign policy around counterterrorism (and, for conspicuous domestic reasons, away from human rights); the war in Iraq; and the global economic crash of 2008. More than a decade later, twenty-two of the forty-four countries furthest away from reaching these goals have experienced, or are experiencing, armed conflict. It is in these environments that women are tortured, brutally raped, have fewer opportunities to attend school, and struggle to assert rights many of us take for granted.

As a woman and a doctor in the middle of these conversations with women and young girls living in extreme circumstances, I have been privy to some extraordinary revelations. The presence of a man in this equation changes the dynamic and, as I have witnessed on many occasions over the years, can cause even the most outspoken and charismatic young women to hesitate. And so while it never stops being annoying to hear someone declare, "You had to be there," what I can offer is that to be a woman in a war zone, surrounded by other women, is to learn and see things I might have missed had I been a tall, imposing male. Because whether I found myself in a pastoral community in a remote stretch of desert in Somalia, or in a walled compound in suburban Kabul breaking bread, there was always one thing that could be relied upon: women, everywhere in the world, *talk*. They talk, often in intimate detail, about marriage, sex, work, children, relationships, politics, history, religion, and community. They talk, even in cultures where they can be stoned to death for their indiscretions. And these experiences have convinced me that the most effective way to break the cycle of poverty and violence is to strategically enhance development assistance to organizations working directly with women to raise their education levels, mobilize communities to increase girls' enrollment and retention at the primary and secondary school levels (and beyond), strengthen women's economic autonomy, and invest in legal mechanisms to end their abuse. Of course, the accessibility of women's reproductive health services (from birth control through to obstetrics and gynecological care), improvements to basic water and sanitation, and the advancement of women in politics and business are essential, but they also logically relate to these other priorities. In particular, education consistently correlates to better health (including lower maternal, infant, and child mortality rates) and economic outcomes for women and children. Based on a landmark study of demographic data from 1970 to 2009, for every additional year of education women of reproductive age in developing countries obtained, the death rate among children under five dropped by 10 percent.

Aid is wasted without improvements to women's education. Even the most effective humanitarian interventions are stymied by high rates of female illiteracy in such countries as Afghanistan and Somalia, where girls' education is often seen as antithetical to religious and social norms. Under such conditions, the value of educating girls is recognized the moment her mother is able to read and write. This is not to suggest that men don't matter (they do), but the cycle of violence and despair that plagues beleaguered nations will not end so long as women remain marginalized by illiteracy and are catastrophically poor. Men must be engaged in this process, in no small measure to ensure that they do not obstruct women's advancement. The most affordable, efficient, and transformational way to prevent conflict and human suffering does not lie in swelling military aid and raising defence budgets. It lies in ensuring that women and girls have choices other than subservience and reproductive surrender.

In 2003, on an arid, dusty evening in Peshawar — a major

centre for trade in textiles, firearms, and narcotics near the Afghan-Pakistan border – I was invited by the Afghan director of an irrepressible local women's organization* to a reception in honour of our forthcoming partnership. Their grassroots programming focused on the thousands of war widows and Afghan refugees living in Pakistan's squalid camps, providing them with holistic support that included medical and psychosocial care, literacy training, and market-based income-generating activities. Many of the women in the program had fled during the decade-long Soviet war in Afghanistan and were raising their children in Peshawar's tent cities, which were overrun with tuberculosis, rats, and violent offenders. Far too many of the women tearfully admitted to having sold one or more of their prepubescent daughters to men they knew to be serial rapists and abusers in order to ensure their youngest children had food to eat. Others had been detained or beaten by Pakistani police or military forces on allegations of prostitution or solicitation, or for refusing to concede to their lascivious advances. Sexual extortion was common, and in an environment where crimes of rape are typically "resolved" by forcing the victim to marry her rapist, Afghan women refugees had all the operability of a fox on the day of the hunt.

With the collapse of the Taliban, refugees were being repatriated to Afghanistan and services to the camps were winding down. Many of the women had even less to return to in Afghanistan than they had in Peshawar, and they were anxious about their security and fearful of the future. To ease them through this transition, the local women's organization planned

---

* In the interest of their safety and security, I have withheld the name of the organization from this publication.

to return to Kabul and continue their programming, helping women reintegrate into Afghan life and equipping them with the skills and education they needed to be financially self-reliant. War Child had offered them support as an international partner, providing both financial resources and training. It was not a hollow offer. Despite their courage and tenacity, the group was widely viewed as having limited capacity[*] and focused on an indigent subsector of Afghan society with long odds: destitute and illiterate women and their children. The group had no other international partners, and there was every reason to believe the initiative would fail. But I'd committed to the women that we would succeed or fail together, and they had convened a group to celebrate.

The women arrived wearing their salwar kameez, their eyes smudged with kohl beneath burqas and hijabs. I was struck by the extent to which the household door represented both a physical and psychological threshold. They arrived covered and subdued, balancing platters of Oorma Nadroo and Bademjan Burani on one hip and a toddler on the other. But once inside, their loose hair fell over their paisley embroidered tops as their hips pulsed to bootlegged tapes of Afghan singers living in exile. After a few embarrassing attempts at dancing, I sat with my legs curled on the kind of flowered, tufted sofa that is the symbol of living room formality across South Asia.

The women shuffled rhythmically between their circles of conversation and a peeling lino-floored kitchen, distributing sweets and shot glasses of tea as the house filled with the warmth

---

[*] As a rare organization run by Afghan women for Afghan women that had been forced to flee the Taliban, they not surprisingly lacked the infrastructure of male-dominated local NGOs.

of cooking and frankincense. They were complex in their duality: at once bold and reserved; progressive in their political opinions but timid about expressing them; hopeful their girls would one day lead more independent lives but resigned to their own fates. Beneath their passion and defiance was a justifiable weariness that their dreams were intangible. To hear them express their views and tell their stories, as an outsider taken into their confidence, was to be left with mixed feelings of solidarity and exasperation. Several times, they openly mocked and derided every facet of the male patriarchy that organized itself around their brutal submission. And yet, on as many occasions, they also talked about the inappropriateness of women walking unaccompanied by a male family member and of finding refuge in the burqa in situations where they could be taunted and leered at. Having experienced the displeasure of being maliciously denounced in the streets of Peshawar and Kabul as a "whore" and an "infidel" with considerable regularity, I understood their desire to deny men the satisfaction. But then, like many women, I've been subjected to equally degrading epithets on the streets of Toronto, New York, and London and have found my middle finger far more liberating than walking around under a bedsheet. The women's movement is unfinished everywhere.

The evening ended with a hilariously awkward moment when one young woman, who was to be married a month later, confessed to feeling anxious about what was going to be her first sexual experience. This sparked a round of intimate testimonials from those in attendance about sex on wedding nights, their husbands' performances (with one woman offering that it is better to be the First Wife marrying a man still in his youth because, "It doesn't last long. You will barely notice"), and other colourful commentary that left absolutely nothing to the imagination.

Now, as a doctor, I don't consider myself to be prudish about anything at all. But I must admit that on this occasion, I was left speechless when all eyes trained on me as I was asked: "What was it like for you, then? The first time you had sex on your wedding night?" How to explain our cultural differences? How to tell them that, like many couples back home, my husband and I had lived together for several years before we were married? And how to politely say it was *none of their business*? Instead, I stammered something along the lines of, "Uh . . . well. You see . . . uh . . . We've been together . . . uh . . . a long time . . ." They stared at me with a combination of pity and disappointment that signalled they thought *I* was the most repressed woman in the room.

With concerted training and support from War Child, the group was able to return to Afghanistan and successfully grow their operations, providing literacy and vocational programming to four hundred women annually, and further benefiting thousands of young children. It has been nothing less than astounding to follow the transformational impact the initiative has had on women's lives. Many of the participants were illiterate when they began, and earned income through begging, or depended on aid agency handouts for their survival. Within a year of entering the program, they were able to start their own businesses, enroll their children in school, and form small groups guaranteeing one another's business loans, which are paid from an interest-free revolving fund. This reduces the pressure on individual women and fosters collaboration. In a climate where women are often prohibited from selling their own products at market, owning property, or controlling their own income, Afghan women with no formal education are making significant strides with modest assistance. Graduates help to identify future participants and provide ongoing mentorship and encouragement as they grow their businesses. The revolving fund has retained 98 percent of its value, as women are highly motivated to return the favour by repaying their loans. At every stage, a woman's unique constraints are considered. Men – from fathers, to husbands, to community leaders – are consulted and engaged to ensure women are not endangered or targeted as a result of their enrollment.

The women who have participated in the program over the past six years are still a long way from achieving full equality. In most households where there is a male family member or extended family member the women are not yet free to make independent decisions or even fully control their own resources. But they are, slowly and in their individual ways, overcoming the barriers of oppression and discrimination and inching forward. Whether those successes are transient or permanent depends entirely on the extent to which Afghan women and the organizations taking bold steps to assist them will be afforded the space to continue: the security space; the political space; the financial space. Official Development Assistance can play a major role in this equation, but only when it is applied consistently and to organizations that can be directly accountable to women and their evolving needs.

Women in Afghanistan, as in many countries around the world (including western democracies), are grossly underrepresented in politics and in business.* There's no question that the institutions – government, corporate, bureaucratic, ideological, and religious – that give rise to such discrimination and inequality, either actively or through willful neglect, must also change from within. But this is precisely why local civil

---

* In 2018, women made up less than 20 percent of the United States House of Representatives and held less than a quarter of the seats in the U.S. Congress. Only 6 percent of Fortune 500 companies are run by women.

society groups, which typically enjoy more legitimacy among women and which grant them greater access and leadership opportunities, deserve ongoing support and consideration. The past decade's shift towards aid consolidation sidelines indigenous agencies by reducing their funding options as well as their autonomy. They begin reacting to external and bureaucratic demands in order to survive, rather than being driven by the needs of their constituencies.

In conflict and post-conflict environments, grassroots organizations are critical to social and political reform, and to the protection of human rights and the promotion of gender equality. The venal warlords and Taliban-sympathizers comfortably seated in Afghanistan's parliament are guaranteed, for as long as they remain in power, to continue their vile persecution of women. But their influence is undermined, both substantially and symbolically, with every girl attending school, every female teacher trained, and every woman able to rise to the rank of community leader in politics, business, academia, or non-profit association. Community-based development organizations are powerful incubators, providing women with a shared vision for their advancement.

While working in Liberia, I was similarly impressed by the number and quality of local women's groups tackling a range of difficult social justice issues, from female genital mutilation (which is practised in Liberia, particularly in rural areas) to spousal property rights. I met dozens of their employees and volunteers, and witnessed their field operations. They were fearless and determined, and rarely concealed their contempt for Charles Taylor. One Liberian female lawyer, who donated her time through a local women's legal aid agency to rape victims, confessed that she held out little hope that judges hearing her cases would not be bought off by male defendants. But, as she explained it to me, "We're setting an example for women. And we are showing the police and the government we are paying attention." A few of these groups received direct funding from United Nations agencies and other international organizations. But most survived on modest (as in a couple of hundred dollars) contributions from local businesses and low-key American church and peace groups who'd learned of them largely through resettled refugees or returning aid workers. The women's movement in Liberia later played a significant role in ending the country's civil war and in forcing Charles Taylor into exile – events that culminated in the election of Africa's first elected female president, Ellen Johnson Sirleaf.

Certainly, there is a fine line between supporting local organizations doing groundbreaking work to advance women's rights and subsuming them altogether with a foreign agenda. To that end, social media tools have been credited in recent years with having a more direct influence over social injustice and oppressive regimes than decades of foreign policy measures or NGO-backed equality movements. This is a specious argument for a few reasons: Facebook, Twitter, texting, and other social media platforms require a minimum level of literacy and infrastructure (one that the majority of women in eastern Congo and Darfur, for example, do not have access to); and, in parts of the world known for their regressive treatment of women, social media–spawned protests in support of women's rights are often abruptly ended by extreme brutality. Social media is merely a tool and not a substitute for door-to-door, grassroots development, which is safer and more accessible for the majority of women in unstable environments.

Less than a month after hundreds of thousands of protesters in Cairo toppled Hosni Mubarak's decaying government, young women gathered in Tahrir Square on the occasion of the one-hundredth anniversary of International Women's Day to denounce their ongoing abuse and harassment by Egyptian men. The women were aggressively confronted as men hurled insults at them and pushed their way through the crowd, only retreating when army officers fired warning shots. The women were protesting, among other proposed legislative changes drafted in the withering euphoria of Egyptian "democracy," women's exclusion from the committee tasked with writing the country's constitutional amendments, which suggested that only men could become president. They were shouted down with cries of "Go home, go wash clothes," and "You are not married. Go find a husband." Eighteen women were arrested, tortured, and subjected to "virginity tests" by police. It was clear that Egyptian women had been invited to stand behind men in the stagger towards freedom, but not in front of them (or even, for that matter, *beside* them). A few days earlier, thousands of women protesting in the Ivory Coast had called on their intransigent president Laurent Gbagbo – who by then had already lost all rights to this title – demanding that he relinquish power to his democratically elected opponent. Some boldly marched without their clothes because an Ivorian curse is reportedly invoked by the killing of a naked woman. Tragically, this demonstration ended when soldiers opened fire, fatally shooting six female demonstrators.

Local women's organizations are critical to the struggle against violence and injustice, and women and girls born into environments hostile to their full and equal participation as citizens have waited long enough. Like all women and girls, they must be able to sleep without fear of abduction; they must be able to walk without fear of rape; and they must be able to live without fear of enslavement. The courageous and tireless local organizations, community leaders, teachers, and journalists working to promote women's social, economic, and educational advancement – to defend their rights and safeguard their futures – are changing the circumstances of women's lives by enabling them to have choices they never thought possible. Given the constant threats women are under around the world, it is at times a quieter revolution than the fall of the Berlin Wall, the end of apartheid in South Africa, or the American women's and civil rights movements. And it is a movement towards equality that requires consistent investment, training, education, and partnership if it is to be successful. When making decisions about who and what to give to, look for organizations and initiatives that directly improve women's lives through community-based development. And recognize that even a small amount of money invested regularly is more likely to achieve lasting results than one-time contributions tied to short-term, emergency interventions.

THE BURDEN OF POVERTY AND UNEMPLOYMENT
One of the most significant and ongoing threats to peace globally is the demographic swell of unemployed, unskilled, and uneducated young men in unstable environments. Among the twenty-five countries experiencing armed conflict within their borders, 60 percent of the population is under the age of thirty.* Many of

---

* In fact, over the past thirty years, virtually all countries (86 percent) that experienced a new civil conflict had populations in which 60 percent were younger than thirty years old.

the young men born into fractured societies struggle to overcome years of missed schooling and are chronically poor. In the shadow of conflict, their collective discontent and social disengagement, combined with the easy availability of small arms, virtually guarantee catastrophe. It is a pattern playing itself out in countless conflict and post-conflict countries worldwide, locking civilians in a recurring cycle of poverty, human misery, and instability.

Perhaps the best evidence of this social unravelling is the correlation between human development and war. The lower a country's ranking on the Human Development Index, the greater the likelihood it is experiencing armed conflict within its borders. Over the past twenty-three years, only 5 percent of the countries rated "very high" on the Human Development Index experienced war within their borders, compared to more than half (54 percent) of those ranked "low." The vast majority (80 percent) were in Africa and Asia, split equally between these two continents. Certainly, we can debate chickens and eggs here: are low levels of social, political, and economic development risk factors for armed conflict, or is the reverse more likely? In the most obvious sense, both are true. Countries wracked by violence struggle to provide their citizens with the basic necessities of life, and so are plagued by low human development. After all, parents do not take their children to school or to medical clinics when they risk being raped or killed along the way. And citizens with few educational and employment opportunities, who watch their children die needlessly and whose lives are, in that Hobbesian way, "poor, nasty, brutish, and short" have many more reasons to wage war than not. Add to this the preponderance of autocratic rulers, military regimes, and corrupted governments operating in unstable regions who are able to liberally crush democratic movements and subvert international law, courtesy of lucrative foreign arms deals, and the question must be asked: Whose interests are best served by the status quo? Certainly not the children forced to shoot their siblings, or the illiterate teenagers trafficking drugs and precious metals on behalf of rebel commanders, or the local human rights advocates buried without fingernails. And it is a ghastly instability that spreads both literally and ideologically, offering up the kind of fodder that religious zealots and half-witted demagogues rely on to deliver a primed audience.

The recruitment tools used by the Taliban, Al-Qaeda, and Al-Shabab are no different from those used by warlords the world over: money, a sense of belonging, and an alternative to victimhood. It is why Afghanistan will never be won militarily. The Taliban and Al-Qaeda are not an "enemy" to be fought on the front lines and defeated tactically. These are pseudo-populist movements, however perverse, which are strengthened by fear, poverty, and anger – anger that mounts with every errant Allied missile, cheated Afghan election, imperialistic misadventure, failed Middle East peace agreement, and unlawful detention. It's easy to dismiss this kind of thinking as liberal apologia. After all, none of the September 11 hijackers were poor, uneducated teens from the battered landscapes of Khartoum, Mogadishu, or the Khyber Pass. Nevertheless, the old Churchillian approach to fighting them on the beaches, in the fields, and on the streets no longer applies. The only way to abort such movements – to strip them of their platform and subsequently their foot soldiers – is to strangle them with arms-control measures and thwart them through youth education, skills training, and employment. And it is an investment that serves all of our interests. "Citizens victimized by genocide or abandoned by the international community," Samantha Power writes in her Pulitzer Prize–winning book *A Problem from Hell*, "do not make good neighbours, as their thirst for vengeance, their irredentism, and their acceptance of violence as a means of generating change can turn them into future threats." More recent research into the psychology and background of jihadists and their families in Afghanistan and Pakistan shows that support for such movements grows when ideology and a sense of deprivation converge. Mounting resentment, in the face of military occupation and non-existent opportunities for personal advancement, are powerful accelerants among both educated *and* uneducated young men and women. While improving educational levels and other quality of life indicators may not diminish the appeal of militant movements in the short term, over time such efforts tend to limit their support and erode their legitimacy.

I've witnessed the transformational impact of carefully planned and administered development programming in many (though admittedly not all) of the world's most combustible corners. Angry young men drifting in and out of armed groups until they are offered a genuine opportunity to catch up on missed schooling and the dream of graduation. The former sex slaves of rebel commanders who, with modest social and educational assistance, are able to secure employment and become advocates in their communities. And yet, globally, we currently spend more than twelve times as much money fighting and killing one another as we do on Official Development Assistance. It is a self-defeating strategy. Would there have been any need for a NATO-led military intervention in Libya in 2011 had there not been such willingness to broker arms deals with one of the world's most deranged despots? In 1985, Britain secretly built a chemical plant in Iraq that was a key component in Saddam Hussein's chemical warfare arsenal – three years before he used poison gases to kill thousands of Iraqi Kurds. Through most of the Soviet war in

Afghanistan, the Taliban were the joyous recipients of American munitions – weapons still in wide circulation. When it comes to war, the defence industry (as evidenced by the exorbitant growth in military spending over the past two decades) has a peculiar capacity to fail upwards.

The overwhelming majority of teenage boys I've met over the years throughout Africa, Asia, and the Middle East who in some form or another voluntarily participated in armed combat (whether as soldiers, porters, smugglers, or recruiters) admitted that they would have made different choices had any been on offer. So why aren't they? Because the prevailing view on this side of the world is that the suffering of those living beyond our borders is the domain of charity; an optional concern, and one that does not implicate us equally, as human beings. We base our decisions surrounding who and what to give to on our own emotional longing – choosing a single child to send to school, collecting toys, or building an orphanage – rather than on measures that might negate the need for such erratic handouts. And we respond in kind only when the raw images of those who are starving, dying, or being otherwise brutalized are so persistent and extreme that they can no longer be ignored (and sometimes, as we have learned in Rwanda and Darfur, not even then). Tragedies recur in part because we do not heed history, and as such we fail to recognize the value of prevention even when the steps that can and should be taken are obvious, consistent, inexpensive, and easily implemented.

There is great resilience, courage, and strength in countries in which none ought to exist; in communities defiled by war, famine, rape, oppression, or extreme poverty. The young men and women maturing in the midst of such violence and hardship can, in less than a generation, become a resource for their communities through education and skills training for a fraction of the cost of our ongoing militarization.

LEGAL AID

A major factor underlying the ongoing abuse, rape, and other gross human rights violations taking place in countries reeling from the effects of armed conflict is a culture of impunity (at both the local and international levels), which is readily exploited by war's profiteers. In the chaos of war and its aftermath, human decency and the rule of law are often interred alongside the skeletal and mutilated remains of dead civilians. Without a functioning system of law and order, as the widespread rape of Congolese women and girls demonstrates, there is a deficit of sticks with which to prevent ongoing violations.

Special war crimes tribunals formed to prosecute those implicated in atrocities in the former Yugoslavia, Sierra Leone, and Rwanda were critical to the peace and reconciliation process, and have given victims both the means and the opportunity to seek justice. And the addition of the International Criminal Court* (the ICC) to the mix of mechanisms available to hold war criminals to account is beginning to resonate, as a string of torturers and thugs have been hauled before the courts in recent years who might otherwise have enjoyed quiet retirement in a seaside South American *barrio*.

Admittedly, the efforts of the ICC have focused primarily on easier gets, such as former Congolese rebel leader Thomas Lubanga, than on the indiscreet bedfellows of the world's most powerful economies. The most glaring exception was the ICC's indictment

---

* The ICC is currently ratified by 114 countries but with some significant omissions, including the United States, India, and China.

in 2009 of Sudanese president Omar al-Bashir for war crimes in connection with the Darfur region. Bashir, the first indicted sitting head of state, has long enjoyed relations with China, India, and Russia. The African Union and the Arab League – both of which include among their members others who could one day face ICC prosecutions of their own – rebuked the ICC's decision, as did many international NGOs, human rights advocates, and a number of my friends and colleagues. They dismissed it as a largely symbolic move, as the court had absolutely no mechanism to enforce the warrant, and they accused the chief prosecutor, Luis Moreno-Ocampo, of grandstanding at the expense of humanitarian operations. In the wake of the announcement, thirteen international organizations, including Save the Children, Oxfam GB, and Médecins Sans Frontières, were promptly expelled from Sudan. A few international aid workers were taken hostage. This was followed by expressions of political concern (which would later prove to be overblown) that the indictment might so inflame Bashir that he would scuttle, among other delicate negotiations, the North-South peace process and the long hoped for referendum on southern secession. In total, it amounted to extraordinary hand-wringing over a notorious despot implicated in the widespread suffering of civilians. Until such time as Bashir is either overthrown in a coup d'état or murdered by one of his cronies, the ICC indictment will serve as a damning reminder to all those prepared to eat from his table that they are feasting on ill-gotten gains and may also be held to account. The indictment was a bold step precisely *because* of its symbolism, and it is indeed possible in the years ahead that judicial mechanisms may prove to be more effective than political processes and foreign diplomacy in holding to account those whose fingerprints are on civilian slaughter.

There will be times when fear of prosecution by the ICC or other international judicial bodies might encourage those guilty of atrocities to cling to power to the bitterest of ends, rather than negotiate a peaceful surrender (Mugabe and Gadhafi are two recent case studies). But to insulate heads of state from prosecution in order to close the books on history and move on would be an act of appalling exceptionalism and a grave injustice to their victims. Their refusal to surrender in the face of international law ought not to set them free.

What appears more morally ambiguous, to me, than judicial muscle-flexing is the application of the "Responsibility to Protect" doctrine to justify any measure of war by either the political Left or Right. First presented in a 2001 report commissioned by the Canadian government, R2P (as it is known in development circles) is a laudable commitment to protect populations from genocide, war crimes, ethnic cleansing, and crimes against humanity. Endorsed by world leaders in 2005, it stipulates that, should peaceful measures such as diplomatic and humanitarian intervention fail, the international community may intervene using coercive actions such as sanctions, prosecution, and, as a last resort, military intervention. R2P ideology has since become part of the revisionist history of the 2003 Iraq War. No Weapons of Mass Destruction were found, Bush and Blair both admitted in their unctuous memoirs, but did the world not owe it to the Iraqi people to overthrow a man so committed to their extermination? These kinds of rationalizations set a dangerous precedent, both for their cultural relativism and for making a moral claim in support of "preventive" war.

When I now reflect on my many trips to Iraq over nearly a decade, there were subtle signs that Saddam's influence was beginning to erode: Internet in the Al Rasheed Hotel, distracted minders who frequently failed to show up, public whispers of discontent – all previously unheard of. By 2003, Saddam's loyalist dogs already appeared to be taking their last, frothing gasps. What might have become of him in the 2011 "Arab Spring"? Conscripts to the Iraqi armed forces had cut and run before, sensing that the tide was not in their favour. And R2P raises other awkward questions that have yet to receive a full hearing: Why Libya, for example, and not Darfur, or Congo, Bahrain, Syria, Zimbabwe, Iran, or North Korea? We'll never know because military intervention under R2P, which lands at the feet of the Security Council, is not so much governed by uniform criteria and consistent processes as it is by political expediency and public appetite. I believe in the fundamental tenets of R2P: when states orchestrate the systematic slaughter of their own people, a swift response is both necessary and required. But does this response include providing military support to unknown elements, such as rebel groups, or taking sides in civil wars? Historically, such experiments do not end well. Without a clearly defined mandate, an open invitation to wage war on "humanitarian" grounds is like giving the genie licence to tell the bottle to go fuck itself.

All of these quagmires underscore the growing and urgent need for training and investment in the legal system, including support for lawyers, paralegals, and judges, in many countries that are attempting to evolve out of conflict – most of them African. In environments where victims currently have no legal recourse, where children can be unlawfully detained, trafficked, or (like Nadine) raped repeatedly, the cycle of violence cannot be interrupted without access to justice. International donor countries, human rights and constitutional lawyers, and the legal community can play a substantial role in helping to build responsible, transparent, and functioning judicial systems in conflict-affected states in particular, and in holding perpetrators to account. But it is a long-term investment, and one that cannot be as easily quantified as the number of blankets distributed, water pumps installed, or patients treated. Effective aid is about so much more than knowing where the money went and what it was spent on. For aid to be truly effective it must do more than plug holes while, if you'll forgive the cliché, the dam keeps on leaking and the holes keep on coming. As long as the deficit surrounding public thinking when it comes to aid and charitable donations remains in place, these broader structural challenges will receive neither the attention nor the resources they critically deserve. The next time you're scanning a charity's gift catalogue, forget the goat – give a lawyer. It might be harder to explain, but it will be worth the effort.

SEARCHING FOR ALTERNATIVES

Since that first landing in Somalia, I have grappled with the same questions. Why is there war? How is it possible that, as human beings – beings capable of so much love and empathy and concern – we can be so recklessly consumed by hate? As our global society becomes increasingly interconnected, and our potential to reach across borders and directly engage one another in rejecting the murderous forces of repression and division is amplified, it is hard to believe that we continue to make such a disproportionate investment in the machinery of our own destruction. Over the past decade there has been an extraordinary if not decisively dangerous focus on military solutions to external threats – both real and perceived. That other options do exist to both prevent such threats and manage their existence, through energized foreign diplomacy and policy, peacekeeping, development innovations, and humanitarian initiative, is rarely discussed as the drums of war beat feverishly louder. Where does the truth lie? In war, it is always evolving and always evasive. What matters is not what we know, but what we *think* we know — the facts as they are repeated, and not as they are dissected through debate and inquiry. War perverts our capacity for reason.

"We must remember," said Walter Lippmann, "that in time of war what is said on the enemy's front is always propaganda, and what is said on our side of the front is truth and righteousness, the cause of humanity and a crusade for peace." Manipulating the message in war is as old as war itself. It is what makes reasonable people in war capable of rape and murder, and unreasonable people capable of inciting such atrocities. And the risk of war to all of us, in the form of future conflicts over rising food prices, natural resources, and drought and displacement brought about by climate change, is escalating. Nine countries (counting an undeclared Israel) now possess nuclear weapons (including the United States, France, Britain, Russia, China, India, Pakistan, and North Korea), and Iran's nuclear ambitions are growing ever stronger. For as long as we fail to question the status quo, we relegate ourselves to a volatile and uncertain future.

THE FIRST OF MANY STEPS: WHAT YOU CAN DO

Social change (anywhere in the world) begins with education. Our collective ability to reject misinformation, challenge assumptions, and explore alternatives is enhanced by reading and by engaging in civic action — whether by voting in elections, participating in thoughtful protest, writing a blog, joining an NGO, running for public office, or attending an open lecture. (At the end of this book, you will find a list of some of the online resources I recommend, which provide outlets for you to continue learning.)

If you care about issues of war and poverty on a global level, it is also critically important to give. When deciding how to help on an individual level, please consider the following:

- Respond to an urgent crisis or disaster because it does save lives, but not exclusively. The ultimate goal of aid should be to make itself redundant. Make an equal investment in development programming that gives local communities the tools and resources they need to be their own architects of change.
- Regular contributions (for example, monthly gifts, even of small amounts) allow for more responsible, thoughtful programming than one-time donations. These give organizations the ongoing financial security to plan, develop, and implement longer-term programs.
- Avoid earmarking your donations. While this is often assumed to be more transparent, in reality it ends up making it difficult for organizations to invest where the needs are: humanitarian crises no longer in the news. If you are giving to an organization, you should have confidence that it will spend your funds wisely.
- Rather than giving to big organizations reliant on a large expatriate infrastructure at the field level, consider lower-profile, small to medium-sized organizations with strong links to the communities they serve. Ask questions: Does the organization work with local partner agencies or communities? What is its commitment to employing national staff in leadership roles at the field level? Does the organization make training at the local level a priority, and what capacity does it leave behind?

- Know how the organization raises money, and consider whether those methods are in line with a respectful, sensitive portrayal of people living with war and poverty, globally. Sometimes this is nothing more than a feeling. A good test is to see how many times you can watch an organization's commercial without cringing. If you find yourself quickly switching it off, you have your answer.

- Ask how much the organization spends on advertising, annually. This is usually in addition to overhead and is calculated separately as a fundraising expense. For your donation to be effective, fundraising expenses (including advertising) *plus* overhead should add up to less than 25 percent of an organization's budget. But overhead *is* needed to promote stability within organizations and their programs, and to attract talent to the sector. Seventy-five cents on the donated dollar well managed is infinitely better than a hundred cents on the dollar wasted. Do not be tempted by requests to donate new or used clothing, books, shoes, toys, etc.

- Invest in promoting an end to violence and instability by giving to organizations that work to change the circumstances of people's lives: education (including adult education), gender equality, economic empowerment, youth employment, the promotion and protection of human rights and international law, skills training initiatives, HIV/AIDS prevention and management – programs that move beyond traditional notions of "charity."

At the national level, another way to give is to lobby for changes to Official Development Assistance (ODA) policy. ODA funding has become a marginal issue, at least politically, since the economic crash of 2008. The next few years will be critical to the future stability of many countries, most of them in Africa and the Middle East. Discussions around achieving the paltry 0.7 percent target for ODA must continue because the consequences of inaction will prove, as they repeatedly do, to be far more costly.

Remember that thoughtful divestment can be a powerful means of registering your concern. Some of the largest public-sector worker funds in Canada and the United States are profiting from the sale of small arms, land mines, cluster bombs, and other military munitions implicated in the abject suffering of human beings. Ironically, many of these same funds have stated "ethical" investment policies. The arguments against ethical investing made by pension fund managers are usually ones of convenience (it's too difficult), profit margins (decisions are made based on annual returns), or specificity (Where is the line in the sand? Is it just arms, or all military hardware?). Individually, we have even greater control over how and with whom we invest. My advice here is the same as my despairing editor's after I spent months bogged down in the detritus of the outline for this book, anguishing over how the chronology of events, personal stories, and thematic bits might all fit together: Pick a place to start and see how far you get. For example, start by divesting from producers of small arms, cluster bombs, nuclear arms, and land mines. And if that works, keep going. The Stockholm International Peace Research Institute, a leading independent research and policy group, compiles an updated listing of the world's top one hundred arms manufacturers (www.sipri.org).

At the retail level, there are growing numbers of fair trade jewellers, clothing companies, and other manufacturers providing consumers with a wide range of choices. On the issue of cell phones and other electronics, the pusillanimous Apple, Nintendo, and the like must make further improvements when it comes to conflict minerals and other resources by accelerating efforts to publish the names of their suppliers, complete their supply chain audits, and improve transparency. This is only one of many steps needed to reduce the violence in eastern Congo, but at least it is in the right direction. It is time they heard from you.

In the end, the most important thing any of us can do is to continue advancing a more inclusive, respectful, and considered world view. Those who play on fear, who practise the politics of division, who fuel nationalistic fervour, and who incite violence and hate are strengthened by ignorance and public resignation. Their power depends on the powerlessness of others, and it is ours to reject.

There are many moments when I wake at night, watch my husband and son as they sleep, and think about the women I've met over the years who want nothing more than this: to be still in the dark, free from the piercing staccato of automatic gunfire, and to not be afraid. Perhaps it is not possible. But perhaps it is.

Nadya's grass mat lay on the sand between two gnarled wooden posts at the back of a stifling classroom. It was unbearably hot, but the women were energized as their teacher pointed to cursive chalk letters on the blackboard and asked them to read aloud. This was my last stop before curfew: a War Child–supported education centre erected in one of Darfur's many displaced people's camps established to house those whose lives had been viciously torn apart by conflict. The war in Darfur, which began in 2003, has killed an estimated 300,000 people and forced 2.7 million people from their homes. Many Darfurians have lived in the camps' temporary squats for what will soon be a decade. The camps, which often house as many as ten thousand people, are frequently raided at night by roving militia groups. With very little remaining tree cover, the thatched shelters are often washed out during the rainy season. Rape is so widespread that women are forced to decide, every time they must walk to collect firewood, who among them will offer herself up as prey. Usually, it is the grandmothers who volunteer to go.

The teacher introduced me to the women as a visitor from Canada, and I quickly exhausted the few words of Arabic I can confidently speak. I then watched from the sidelines as she continued her lesson. During the day, the centre ran educational programs for children and youth who had missed years of schooling due to war, making it possible for them to re-enter at the appropriate grade level. In the evenings, it was transformed into an adult learning space, where classes were offered to both men and women nightly for six months, focusing on basic literacy and numeracy. The teachers, all Darfurian, were deeply committed to their work and equally grateful for the modest salary.

Nadya was young: twenty-two, she thought, but she couldn't be sure. As the class concluded, a teaching assistant gamely translated as I spoke with some of the participants preparing to leave. Nadya had been in the program for a couple of months, she explained, and was the single mother to a little boy. The rest of her story was deeply familiar to most Darfurian women. She had been in her rural village one afternoon when helicopter gunships furiously approached and opened fire. Villagers scrambled. Her mother, father, and husband shouted to her to grab her newborn son (and only child), and to hide in the thicket behind their family home. She crouched there, loosely concealed, frantically nursing her baby so that he might not cry out – so that they might live. Then she heard the menacing battle cries of the Janjaweed militia.

These veritable horsemen of the apocalypse then launched their assault, and Nadya's small village was overtaken by screams, rape, automatic gunfire, and merciless killings. Throats were slit as villagers begged for mercy. Women and young girls were gang-raped as their husbands and fathers were made to watch, right before they were slaughtered. Children were shot in the back as they ran towards their parents for protection. It was a horrific scene of irrational brutality.

Nadya kept hiding as the Janjaweed arrived at her home. Her father and husband approached them, offering money, food, supplies – pleading to be spared. They were shot dead without warning. Her mother was then dragged from their home, screaming, before they shot her at close range. Nadya watched through the dust and smoke and chaos as her family was ripped apart and decimated. Before leaving, the Janjaweed set fire to her home.

Those who survived did not have time to bury their loved ones. Mostly women and children, they collected whatever remained of their possessions and began the long walk to town. When she arrived at the camp, Nadya told me, she was overwhelmed with grief and deeply afraid. And like more than half of all women in Darfur, Nadya was illiterate, so she struggled to barter her few remaining assets for food and supplies for herself and her son. She didn't understand numbers and couldn't do the simplest mathematical calculations.

Over the past sixteen years, I've listened to too many heart-wrenching stories like Nadya's, stories that left me consumed with grief and anger, and a sense of absolute powerlessness in the face of tyranny. How can this happen? And how can it keep happening, again and again? *On meurt pour rien.*

As I sat beside Nadya and watched the women gently coax one another towards the door, their loose head scarves catching the faintest evening breeze, I wrestled with the same doubts that have plagued me since Somalia. In the face of everything confronting these women – lawlessness, injustice, the insufferable proliferation of arms, sexual persecution, a government implicated in the destruction of its own people, a UN operation that could not effectively protect them – what was the point of programs such as these? It seemed like a useless exercise, one that assuaged western guilt while the atrocities continued.

As I slowly collected my thoughts, I turned to Nadya with one final question: "Nadya," I asked, "after everything you have been through, has any of this helped you?"

She was silent. Then, leaning forward from her mat, she placed her finger in the sand and gently wrote her name. Her long strokes twisted and coiled back on themselves, filling the space between us. When she was finished, she turned to me and said, "Now that I know how to write my own name, I'm going to learn how to write my son's name."

ACKNOWLEDGEMENTS

This book is a culmination of what will soon be two decades of my work in the field of war and human rights, and there are many to whom I am indebted for both tolerating and encouraging me throughout the writing process. I'd like to thank Doug Pepper of McClelland & Stewart (M&S) and my agent Michael Levine for believing that I had something to say and was capable of turning it into a book. As a first-time author, I greatly appreciated the expertise and guidance of my editor, Philip Rappaport, as well as that of Dan Bortolotti, who provided thoughtful edits of early drafts. I would still be in the library and nowhere close to completion were it not for my extraordinary researchers for this book and its updates, Sarah Mikhaiel, Shannon Sutton and François Kenny, who dedicated countless hours to scrounging for information, much of it obscure. A good deal of the data needed for this book, such as information on arms manufacturers and pension funds, is deliberately difficult to find, and their tenaciousness greatly enhanced the final product. Special thanks and sincere apologies go to those who read my earliest drafts and managed to find the right measure of wit, criticism, and reassurance to keep me going; in particular, thank you to Alyson Rowe and James Topham.

I'd like to thank the student volunteers, Michelle MacInnes-Rae, Ani Mamikon, and Jordan Michaux, who helped with additional research requests; Catherine Marjoribanks and Morgan

Jaques for their meticulous review of the final copy; and Josh Glover and the staff at M&S for their hard work and dedication in promoting this book. Nicholas Garrison's help producing an outline was invaluable. Trena White, thank you for bringing me to M&S. Credit also goes to Scott Beveridge and Lorna Read for shouldering part of my day-to-day workload so that I might have the time and space to write. To the staff at Women's College Hospital and War Child, and my patients, thank you for enduring my frequent absences during this process. And, of course, before there can be words on a page there must be supportive teachers, and I want to acknowledge all those whose classrooms I sat in over the years, especially my writing teachers: Nancy Wigston and the late Professor Sylvia Bowerbank. I am also profoundly grateful to Susan Dowswell and Mary Lowery – you stuck me on a stage when I lacked the courage to audition, and taught me to speak my mind boldly and thoughtfully. Teachers change lives every day throughout the world, and I am no exception.

For ideas to work they must be incubated and then shared, and in this respect I consider it one of my greatest privileges to have learned from many of the most critical minds in the sphere of international humanitarian assistance – including my husband, Eric Hoskins; Nigel Fisher; James Orbinski; and the late Pierce Gerety, among others. And I want to thank all those whose stories are told within these pages for sharing their experiences with me and for teaching me that there is always hope, and that it is worth pursuing.

To my family and friends, I would have had neither the capacity to take this on nor the confidence to do so without your persistent faith in me, guidance, and support. Chantal Kreviazuk, Raine Maida, Jenn Gould, Fiona Hack, Gabrielle Duchesne, Jennifer Pitt-Lainsbury, Barbara Harmer, Denise Donlon, Mike

Eizenga, April Franco, Elliot Pobjo, Murray McLauchlan, Seamus O'Regan, Nils Engelstad, Shelley Ambrose, Doug Knight, and the Italy Crew: your friendship saw me through many a difficult moment while writing. I'd never have the time to write if it were not for Sharon Bartholomew, Holly Evenden and Anna Dobie. I owe a great debt to my mother, Joan, and my father, Phillip – who are both Nutts – for creating the kind of family environment where humour, debate, and stubborn persistence were valued. To my sister Pippa and her partner Sean Kenalty, thank you for being a constant source of laughter and happiness in my life.

And so this book closes in the manner in which it opened. To Eric and Rhys, three better words do not exist, so I shall end with them here: I love you.

RECOMMENDED LINKS

AlertNet
   http://www.trust.org/alertnet
Amnesty International
   http://www.amnesty.org
Cluster Munition Coalition
   http://www.stopclustermunitions.org
Control Arms
   http://www.controlarms.org
Dignitas International
   http://www.dignitasinternational.org
Doctors Without Borders
   http://www.doctorswithoutborders.org
Engineers Without Borders Canada
   http://www.ewb.ca
Engineers Without Borders International
   http://www.ewb-international.org
Enough Project
   http://www.enoughproject.org
Global Witness
   http://www.globalwitness.org
Grameen Bank
   http://www.grameenfoundation.org
Human Rights Watch
   http://www.hrw.org

International Campaign to Ban Landmines
   http://www.icbl.org
MiningWatch Canada
   http://www.miningwatch.ca
OneWorld
   http://www.oneworld.net
Oxfam International
   http://www.oxfam.org
Partners in Health
   http://www.pih.org
Project Ploughshares
   http://www.ploughshares.ca
ReliefWeb
   http://www.reliefweb.int
Small Arms Survey
   http://smallarmssurvey.org
Stockholm International Peace Research Institute
   http://www.sipri.org
The Child Soldier Initiative
   http://childsoldiersinitiative.org
The Stephen Lewis Foundation
   http://www.stephenlewisfoundation.org
Unicef
   http://www.unicef.org
War Child Canada
   http://www.warchild.ca
War Child International
   http://www.warchild.org
World University Service of Canada
   http://www.wusc.ca

NOTES

PREFACE

XV   EIGHTY PERCENT In order, these were: the United States ($9.9 billion); Russia ($6.4 billion); Germany ($2.8 billion); France ($2.2 billion); China ($2.1 billion); England ($1.4 billion). Two of these countries, Russia and China, have a shameful history of underreporting the true extent of their arms sales. Stockholm International Peace Research Institute, (Arms Transfer Database). www.SIPRI.org (accessed May 1, 2018).

XV   THIS GROWTH IN SALES Stockholm International Peace Research Institute, (Arms Transfer Database). www.SIPRI.org (accessed May 1, 2018).

XVI   A MORE PLAUSIBLE EXPLANATION Thomas Gibbons-Neff, "U.S. Failed to Keep Proper Track of More Than $1 Billion in Weapons and Equipment in Iraq," *Washington Post*, May 24, 2017, https://www.washingtonpost.com/news/checkpoint /wp/2017/05/24/u-s-failed-to-keep-proper-track-of-more-than- 1-billion-in-weapons-and-equipment-in-iraq/?utm_term=. a86cec6e0ed0; Thomas Gibbons-Neff, "Afghanistan May Have Lost Track of More Than 200,000 Weapons," *Washington Post*, July 28, 2014, https://www.washingtonpost.com/news /checkpoint/wp/2014/07/28/afghanistan-may-have-lost-track- of-more-than-200000-weapons/?utm_term=.78e2eeef7e10.

XVII It was the Obama Administration Paul McLeary "The Pentagon Wasted $500 Million Training Syrian Rebels" *Foreign Policy*, March 18, 2016, http://foreignpolicy.com/2016/03/18/pentagon-wasted-500-million-syrian-rebels/.

XIX KBR is a former Halliburton subsidiary Commission on Wartime Contracting in Iraq and Afghanistan, *Transforming Wartime Contracting: Controlling costs, reducing risks* (August 2011), 23, https://cybercemetery.unt.edu/archive/cwc/20110929213820/http://www.wartimecontracting.gov/docs/CWC_FinalReport-lowres.pdf; David E. Rosenbaum, "A Closer Look at Cheney and Halliburton" *New York Times*, September 28, 2004, https://www.nytimes.com/2004/09/28/us/a-closer-look-at-cheney-and-halliburton.html.

XIX The veracity of these claims Izzat Ibrahim al-Douri, Saddam Hussein's former top deputy, and the two sons of his half-brother Sabawai Ibrahim al-Tikriti (Ayman and Ibrahim Sabawai), alongside other former Ba'athists, aligned themselves with ISIS early in their rise. Tim Arango "Top Saddam Hussein Aide Reported Killed in Northern Iraq," *New York Times*, April 17, 2015, https://www.nytimes.com/2015/04/18/world/middleeast/saddam-hussein-aide-izzat-ibrahim-al-douri-reported-killed.html; Isabel Coles and Ned Parker, "How Saddam's Men Help Islamic State Rule," *Reuters*, December 11, 2015, https://www.reuters.com/investigates/special-report/mideast-crisis-iraq-islamicstate/.

XXVI Eventually, the *Toronto Star* and ABC News Mitch Potter, Michelle Shephard and Bruce Campion-Smith, "Bound. Tortured. Killed," *Toronto Star*, May 25, 2017, http://projects.thestar.com/iraq-torture-abuse-murder-war-crimes/.

XXVII Human Rights Watch later would report "KRG: Children Allege Torture by Security Forces," *Human Rights*

Watch, January 29, 2017, https://www.hrw.org/news/2017
/01/29/krg-children-allege-torture-security-forces.

XXVIII THESE KINDS OF RECOVERY PROGRAMS Centre for International
Cooperation and Security, *Disarmament, Demobilisation and
Reintegration in Sierra Leone (July 2008).* http://www.
operationspaix.net/DATA/DOCUMENT/4024~v~
Disarmament_Demobilisation_and_Reintegration_in_Sierra_
Leone.pdf.

INTRODUCTION

1   I WAS TRAVELLING WITH A DOCUMENTARY CREW to co-produce
a documentary later titled *Rocked: Sum 41 in Congo.* Our team
included Sum 41 band members Deryck Whibley, Dave Baksh,
Cone McCaslin, and Steve Jocz, road manager Jeff Marshall, and
logistician and translator Daisy Njebenjek. *Rocked* was produced
by Eric Hoskins, Samantha Nutt, and Barbara Harmer; directed
and edited by George Vale; and directed and co-produced by
Adrian Callender. We were evacuated from The Orchid together
in May 2004. *Rocked: Sum 41 in Congo*, directed by Adrian
Callender and George Vale, distributed by War Child Canada,
2005. Studio: Universal Music Group.

8   Mehdi Hasan, "US Drone Attacks Are No Laughing Matter,
Mr Obama," *Guardian*, December 28, 2010,
http://www.guardian.co.uk/commentisfree/cifamerica/2010
/dec/28/us-drone-attacks-no-laughing-matter.

12   War Child Canada founders also include Steven Hick, author
and professor of Social Work at Carlton University, and notable
Canadian philanthropist Frank O'Dea as founding Chair.
My husband, Eric Hoskins, who joined War Child in 2001,
was instrumental in the organization's vision and growth

during the critical early years, and is now formally
acknowledged as a Founder.

14   BOB GELDOF'S CONCERT Peter Walker and Daniel Maxwell, eds.,
      Shaping the Humanitarian World (New York: Routledge, 2009).

CHAPTER 1

18   BAIDOA: THE CITY OF DEATH Freedom House, "Freedom in
      the World 2009 – Somalia," http://www.unhcr.org/refworld
      /docid/4a645283c.html (accessed May 19, 2011).

22   SOMALIA HAS HAD World Health Organization, "Part I: Health
      Related Millennium Development Goals," Geneva, World
      Health Organization, 26, http://www.who.int/whosis
      /whostat/EN_WHS10_Part1.pdf.

26   IN TOTAL, 37,000 INTERNATIONAL TROOPS Walter Clarke and
      Jeffrey Herbst, eds., *Learning from Somalia: Lessons of Armed
      Humanitarian Intervention* (Boulder: Westview Press, 1997), 153.

26   WHILE EXPERTS ARGUED Mohamed Sahnoun, *Somalia:
      The Missed Opportunities* (Washington, D.C.: U.S. Institute of
      Peace Press, 1994), xiii.

26   CLINTON NEEDED NO CONVINCING "The Somalia Mission;
      Clinton's Words on Somalia: 'The Responsibilities of
      American Leadership,'" *New York Times*, October 8, 1993,
      http://www.nytimes.com/1993/10/08/world/somalia
      -mission-clinton-s-words-somalia-responsibilities-american
      -leadership.html.

27   'I BELIEVE IN KILLING' George Stephanopoulus, *All Too Human:
      A Political Education* (New York: Little, Brown and Company,
      1999), 214.

32   BOTH THE LTTE AND THE SRI LANKAN GOVERNMENT
      United Nations, *Report of the Secretary-General's Panel of*

Experts on Accountability in Sri Lanka (March, 2011), 115, http://www.un.org/News/dh/infocus/Sri_Lanka/POE _Report_Full.pdf.

32 IN RECENT YEARS, THE COMBINED Stockholm International Peace Research Institute, "Top 100 Arms-Producing and Military Services Companies," December 2017, https://www. sipri.org/sites/default/files/2017-12/fs_arms_industry_2016.pdf.

33 EVERY YEAR, 8 MILLION Small Arms Survey, "Weapons and Markets," http://www.smallarmssurvey.org/weapons-and -markets.html (accessed May 19, 2011); Small Arms Survey, *Small Arms Survey 2003: Development Denied* (Oxford: Oxford University Press, 2003),13, http://www.smallarmssurvey.org /fileadmin/docs/A-Yearbook/2003/en/Small-Arms-Survey -2003-Chapter-01-EN.pdf.

33 CANADA, WHICH IS AMONG The Small Arms Survey "Small Arms Trade Transparency Barometer," 2017, http://www. smallarmssurvey.org/fileadmin/docs/Weapons_and_Markets /Tools/Transparency_barometer/SAS-Transparency- Barometer-2017.pdf.

33 TO THAT END Stockholm International Peace Research Institute, "Top 100 Arms-Producing and Military Services Companies," December 2017, https://www.sipri.org/sites /default/files/2017-12/fs_arms_industry_2016.pdf.

33 CHINA DOESN'T PRODUCE RELIABLE DATA Stockholm International Peace Research Institute "TIV of arms exports from China 2005–2008," (Arms Transfer Database), www.SIPRI.org (accessed January 11, 2010).

34 CIVIL LIBERTIES ACTIVISTS *Washington Times*, "The U.N. Gun Grabber: Global Small Arms Treaty Threatens Your Right to Self Defense," May 27, 2010, http://www.washingtontimes.com /news/2010/may/27/the-un-gun-grabber.

35   IT'S A WORRISOME PATTERN *Telegraph*, "Most US aid to Egypt goes to military," January 29, 2011, http://www.telegraph.co.uk /finance/financetopics/8290133/Most-US-aid-to-Egypt-goes -to-military.html.

35   IT'S A WORRISOME PATTERN Joby Warrick, "U.S. steps up arms sales to Persian Gulf allies," *Washington Post*, January 31, 2010, http://www.washingtonpost.com/wp-dyn/content/article /2010/01/30/AR2010013001477.html.

35   IT'S A WORRISOME PATTERN William D. Hartung and Frida Berrigan, "US Weapons at War 2008: Beyond the Bush Legacy," *New America Foundation*, December 2008, http:// www.newamerica.net/publications/policy/u_s_weapons_ war_2008_0; Thalif Deen, "Uncertain Fate for Egypt's U.S.-Supplied Weapons Systems," *Inter Press Service*, January 28, 2011, http://ipsnews.net/news.asp?idnews=54280.

36   IN THE MONTHS BEFORE Stephen Braun, Associated Press, "Before Libya's Turmoil, U.S. Planned Arms Sale," *The World*, March 7, 2011, http://theworldlink.com/news/local/article _d7a036a4-7b2f-53ae-afe8-869bbd170903.html.

36   AND WHY SHOULDN'T THEY? *Guardian*, "EU arms exports to Libya: who armed Gaddafi?" http://www.guardian.co.uk /news/datablog/2011/mar/01/eu-arms-exports-libya (accessed May 31, 2011).

36   A FEW YEARS LATER Michelle Nichols, "Libya Arms Fueling Conflicts in Syria, Mali and beyond: U.N. experts," *Reuters*, April 9, 2013, https://www.reuters.com/article/us-libya-arms-un/libya-arms-fueling-conflicts-in-syria-mali-and-beyond-u-n-experts-idUSBRE93814Y20130409.

36   AMONG THE WORLD'S POOREST UNESCO, *EFA Global Monitoring Report: The Hidden Crisis: Armed Conflict and Education*

(UNESCO: 2011), 2, http://unesdoc.unesco.org/images
/0019/001907/190743e.pdf.

36   AT THE START OF 2010 Ontario Teachers' Pension Plan,
"2009 Annual Report: Taking Care of Business," 106,
http://docs.otpp.com/AnnualReport.pdf.

36   THE NEW YORK STATE AND CALIFORNIA STATE New York
State Teachers' Retirement System, *Domestic Equity Holdings as
of December 31, 2017*, https://www.nystrs.org/NYSTRS/media
/PDF/About%20Us/equity_domestic.pdf (accessed May 25,
2018); California State Teachers' Retirement System, *Domestic
Equities as of June, 30, 2017*, https://www.calstrs.com/
investment-table/domestic-equities (accessed August 16, 2017).

37   THE CANADA PENSION PLAN (CPP) Canadian Pension Plan
Investment Board, *Foreign Publicly-Traded Equity Holdings As
of March 31st, 2017*, http://www.cppib.com/documents/1606/
foreign_publicequityholdings_Mar2017_en.htm; Canadian
Pension Plan Investment Board, *Canadian Publicly-Traded Equity
Holdings As of March 31st, 2017*, http://www.cppib.com/
documents/1604/cdn_publicequityholdings_Mar2017_en.htm.
These figures were derived by comparing CPP holdings to
SIPRI's list of top one hundred arms-producing companies.

44   EVEN AFTER AN ARMS EMBARGO Associated Press, "UN Report
Says 10 Nations Violating Arms Embargo," *Global Policy Forum*,
November 15, 2006, http://www.globalpolicy.org/component
/content/article/205-somalia/39457.html.

44   DURING THE 2010 WORLD CUP Max Delany, "Uganda Bombings:
Somalis in Uganda's Capital Now Fear Reprisal Attack," *Christian
Science Monitor*, July 13, 2010, http://www.csmonitor.com/World
/Africa/2010/0713/Uganda-bombings-Somalis-in-Uganda-s-
capital-now-fear-reprisal-attacks.

CHAPTER 2

48   DURING THE THIRTY-TWO YEARS THAT MOBUTU Steve Askin, "Zaire's Den Of Thieves," *New Internationalist*, June 1990, http://www.newint.org/features/1990/06/05/den.

48   BY 1998, THE NEWLY RENAMED DRC David Mugnier, "North Kivu: How to End a War," *Open Democracy*, December 3, 2007, http://www.opendemocracy.net/article/africa_democracy /congo_north_kivu.

48   THE CONFLICT FORCED MILLIONS International Rescue Committee, "IRC Study Shows Congo's Neglected Crisis Leaves 5.4 Million Dead; Peace Deal in N. Kivu, Increased Aid Critical to Reducing Death Toll," January 22, 2008, http://www.rescue.org/news/irc-study-shows-congos -neglected-crisis-leaves-54-million-dead-peace-deal-n-kivu -increased-aid--4331.

49   IN 2000, MORE THAN 5,000 BBC, "Timeline: Democratic Republic of Congo," http://news.bbc.co.uk/2/hi/africa /country_profiles/1072684.stm (accessed May 17, 2011).

50   BETWEEN 60 AND 80 PERCENT Global Witness, *Under-Mining Peace: The Explosive Trade in Casserite in Eastern DRC* (June, 2005), 13, http://www.globalwitness.org/sites/default/files/pdfs /Under-Mining%20Peace.pdf; BBC, "Miners Buried in DR Congo," January 15, 2002, http://news.bbc.co.uk/2/hi /africa/1761540.stm.

50   AS IS THE CASE FOR MANY GIRLS UNICEF, *The State of the World's Children 2011: Adolescence an Age of Opportunity* (New York: UNICEF, February 2011), 104, http://www.unicef.org /sowc2011/pdfs/SOWC-2011-Main-Report_EN_02092011.pdf.

54   IT HAS BECOME A KIND Jonathan Clayton and James Bone, "Sex Scandal in Congo Threatens to Engulf UN's

Peacekeepers," *Times* (London), December 23, 2004, http://www.timesonline.co.uk/tol/news/world/article405213.ece.

54   THE CONGO, FOR ALL United Nations Organization Mission in Democratic Republic of the Congo, "MONUC Facts and Figures," http://www.un.org/en/peacekeeping/missions/monuc/facts.shtml (accessed June 2, 2011).

54   THIS AREA IS ALSO HOME Iain Marlow and Omar El Akkad, "Smartphones: Blood Stains at Our Fingertips," *Globe and Mail*, December 3, 2010, http://www.theglobeandmail.com/news/technology/smartphones-blood-stains-at-our-fingertips/article1825207/page1.

54   WHEN THEY PLOTTED THE LOCATION Denis Mukengere Mukwege and Cathy Nangin, "Rape with Extreme Violence: The New Pathology in South Kivu, Democratic Republic of Congo," Public Library of Science 6, no. 12, (December 2009), http://www.plosmedicine.org/article/info%3Adoi%2F10.1371%2Fjournal.pmed.1000204.

54   WHETHER IT WAS *The Economist*, "A Jungle Alliance That May Just Endure," March 5, 2009, http://www.economist.com/node/13240217.

55   THE ENOUGH PROJECT The Enough Project, *A Comprehensive Approach to Congo's Conflict Minerals* (April 3, 2009), http://www.enoughproject.org/publications/comprehensive-approach-conflict-minerals-strategy-paper.

55   FOR EXAMPLE, IN 2016 Massachusetts Institute of Technology *Where Does Rwanda Export Niobium, Tantalum, Vanadium and Zirconium Ore To?* (2016), https://atlas.media.mit.edu/en/visualize/tree_map/hs92/export/rwa/show/2615/2016/.

55   MEANWHILE, UGANDA, WHICH DOMESTICALLY PRODUCES Enough: The Project to End Genocide and Crimes Against

Humanity, *Breaking the Cycle: Delinking Armed Actors from the Gold Supply Chain in Congo and the Great Lakes Region Through Fiscal Reform and Anti-Money Laundering* (May 2017), https://enoughproject.org/wp-content/uploads/2017/05/BreakingTheCycle_April2017_Enough_3.pdf

55   WHILE IT IS DIFFICULT TO KNOW Nadira Lalji, "The Resource Curse Revised: Conflict and Coltan in the Congo," *Harvard International Review*, 2007, https://www.globalpolicy.org/the-dark-side-of-natural-resources-st/water-in-conflict/40150.html.

56   THIS RELATIONSHIP SIMPLY World Bank, *Democratic Republic of Congo Growth with Governance in the Mining Sector* (May 2008), 6. http://siteresources.worldbank.org/INTOGMC/Resources/336099-1156955107170/drcgrowthgovernanceenglish.pdf.

56   IN ALLOWING THE RAMPANT USE Based on value of Canadian assets up to 2009. Geoffrey York, "The High Cost of Doing Business with Undemocratic Regimes," *Globe and Mail*, March 21, 2011, http://www.theglobeandmail.com.

56   In 2010, KABILA'S GOVERNMENT GREW TIRED Oxford Analytica, "Eastern Insecurity Dents Kabila Image, *ReliefWeb*, August 18, 2010, http://reliefweb.int/node/364528.

57   WHILE COMPETITION FOR THE CONGO'S MINING Delany (see chap. 1, n. 25).

57   IN RECENT YEARS, NOKIA . . . Ibid.

58   OVER 75 PERCENT Foreign Affairs and International Trade Canada, "Building the Canadian Advantage: A Corporate Social Responsibility (CSR) Strategy for the Canadian International Extractive Sector," March 2009, http://www.international.gc.ca/trade-agreements-accords-commerciaux/ds/csr-strategy-rse-stategie.aspx.

58   OVER HALF MiningWatch Canada, "Suppressed Report Confirms International Violations by Canadian Mining

Companies," news release, October 18, 2010, http://www.
miningwatch.ca/en/suppressed-report-confirms-international-
violations-canadian-mining-companies.

58 OVER 75 PERCENT Marlow and El Akkad.

58 CANADA'S MINING SECTOR MiningWatch Canada, "Bill C-300 a
High Water Mark for Mining and Government Accountability,"
news release, November 15, 2010, http://www.miningwatch.ca
/en/bill-c-300-high-water-mark-mining-and-government
-accountability.

59 GUIDED BY THE EXPERIENCES Bill Curry, "G20 Leaders Signal
Move from Aid to Business," Globe and Mail, June 7, 2010,
http://www.theglobeandmail.com/news/world/g8-g20/news
/g20-leaders-signal-move-from-aid-to-business/article1594676/.

62 IN SIERRA LEONE, FOR EXAMPLE The Enough Project, A
Comprehensive Approach to Congo's Conflict Minerals (April 3, 2009),
http://www.enoughproject.org/publications/comprehensive
-approach-conflict-minerals-strategy-paper; Foundation for
Environmental Security & Sustainability, Reclaiming the Land
After Mining: Improving Environmental Management and Mitigating
Land-Use Conflicts in Alluvial Diamond Fields in Sierra Leone
(USAID, July 2007), http://www.fess-global.org/Publications
/Other/Reclaiming_the_Land_After_Mining.pdf.

62 ALTHOUGH THE LAW DOESN'T BAN Mary Beth Sheridan,
"U.S. Financial Reform Bill Also Targets 'Conflict
Minerals' from Congo," Washington Post, July 21, 2010,
http://www.washingtonpost.com/wp-dyn/content
/article/2010/07/20/AR2010072006212.html.

62 THIS LED TO THE CREATION ITRI, "Conflict Free Smelter
Program," http://www.itri.co.uk/pooled/articles/BF
_NEWSART/view.asp?Q=BF_NEWSART_321655
(accessed June 1, 2011).

63   As GOOGLE DEMONSTRATED BBC, "Google Stops Censoring
      Search Results in China," March, 23, 2010, http://news.bbc
      .co.uk/2/hi/business/8581393.stm.

CHAPTER 3

68   ON MARCH 20, 2003 Robert Fisk, "Bombing the Phone System:
      Another Little Degradation," *Counterpunch*, March 29, 2003,
      http://www.counterpunch.org/fisk03292003.html.

68   BY THE END The number of Iraqis killed was calculated
      based on estimates that 30 percent of Iraqis were killed
      in the invasion phase (before May 1, 2003) from a total
      of 24,865 Iraqis killed during the first two years of the war.
      Similarly, the number of Iraqis injured was calculated based
      on estimates that 41 percent of Iraqis were injured in the
      invasion phase (before May 1, 2003) from a total of 42,000
      civilians wounded during the first two years. Iraq Body
      Count, "A Dossier of Civilian Casualties in Iraq 2003–2005,"
      http://www.iraqbodycount.org/analysis/reference/press
      -releases/12 (accessed May 21, 2011).

69   Central Intelligence Agency, "Iraq Economic Data
      (1989–2003): Regime Finance and Procurement –
      Annex D," https://www.cia.gov/library/reports/general
      -reports-1/iraq_wmd_2004/chap2_annxD.html (accessed
      June 25, 2011).

71   ONE DIRGE SUNG BY SCHOOLCHILDREN Associated Press, "Iraq
      Leader: 'One Who Confronts,'" *Los Angeles Times*, August 4,
      1990, http://articles.latimes.com/1990-08-04/news
      /mn-1057_1_president-saddam-hussein.

71   THE U.S.-LED FORCES U.S. Congress, House, United States
      Government Accountability Office, *Testimony before the Committee*

on Government Reform, 109th Cong., 2006, H. Rep. GAO-06 -1130T, 3, http://www.gao.gov/new.items/d061130t.pdf.

71   Central Intelligence Agency, "Iraq Economic Data (1989–2003): Regime Finance and Procurement – Annex D," https://www.cia.gov/library/reports/general-reports-1 /iraq_wmd_2004/chap2_annxD.html (accessed June 25, 2011).

72   MARGARET WAS, AS *THE GUARDIAN* ONCE DESCRIBED HER, "Margaret Hassan, Relief Worker Who Dedicated Her Life to Helping the Iraqi People," *Guardian*, November 17, 2004, http://www.guardian.co.uk/society/2004/nov/17 /internationalaidanddevelopment.guardianobituaries.

76   "I THINK THIS IS A VERY HARD CHOICE" Madeleine Albright, interview by Amy Goodman, *Democracy Now! Confronts Madeleine Albright on the Iraq Sanctions: Was It Worth The Price?* June 30, 2004, http://www.democracynow.org/2004/7/30/democracy_ now_confronts_madeline_albright_on.

77   FOR THE PAST TWO DECADES Mary Kaldor, *New and Old Wars: Organized Violence in a Global Era* (California: Stanford University Press, 2007), 107.

83   HEEDING THE CALL BBC, "Karbala and Najaf: Shia Holy Cities," April 20, 2003, http://news.bbc.co.uk/2/hi /middle_east/2881835.stm.

86   AID IS EVEN DESCRIBED U.S. Army Combined Arms Center, *Commander's Guide to Money as a Weapons System: Tactics, Techniques and Procedures* (April 2009), 13, http://cgsc.contentdm.oclc. org/cdm4/item_viewer.php?CISOROOT=/p15040co1114&CIS OPTR=8&CISOBOX=1&REC=5.

86   BETWEEN 2002 AND 2005 OECD, "United States (2006), DAC Peer Review: Main Findings and Recommendations," http://www.oecd.org/document/27/0,3746,en_2649_34603 _37829787_1_1_1_1,00.html (accessed May 21, 2011).

87   PRT EFFORTS IN AFGHANISTAN Rod Nordland, "Killings of
      Afghan Relief Workers Stir Debate," *New York Times*, December
      13, 2010, http://www.nytimes.com/2010/12/14/world
      /asia/14afghan.html.

87   CANADIAN, GERMAN, AMERICAN, AND SWEDISH Caroline
      Wyatt, "Is NATO Losing the War in Afghanistan?" BBC,
      August 13, 2010, http://www.bbc.co.uk/news/mobile
      /world-south-asia-10962827.

87   CANADIAN, GERMAN, AMERICAN AND SWEDISH Nordland,
      "Killings of Afghan Relief Workers Stirs Debate."

87   AND PRT SCHOOLS ARE SEEN Marit Glad, *Knowledge on Fire:
      Attacks on Education in Afghanistan: Risks and Measures for
      Successful Mitigation* (CARE: November 2009), 25.

88   JUST OVER HALF OF CERP FUNDS Special Inspector General
      for Afghanistan Reconstruction, *Quarterly Report for the United
      States Congress*, October 2009, 46, http://www.sigar.mil/pdf
      /quarterlyreports/Oct09/pdf/SIGAROct2009Web.pdf.

88   IN ADDITION, CERP FUNDING Sippi Azarbaijani-Moghaddam,
      Mirwais Wardak, Idrees Zaman, and Annabel Taylo, *Afghan
      Hearts, Afghan Minds: Exploring Afghan Perceptions of Civil-military
      Relations* (European Network of NGOs in Afghanistan and the
      British and Irish Agencies Afghanistan Group, 2008), 8,
      http://www.humansecuritygateway.com/documents
      /ENNA_BAAG_Afghanistan_afghanheartsafghanminds.pdf.

88   THE U.S. GOVERNMENT ACCOUNTABILITY OFFICE Office of the
      Special Inspector General for Iraq Reconstruction (SIGIR),
      *Statement of Stuart W. Bowen, Jr., Special Inspector General for Iraq
      Reconstruction before the United States Senate Committee on Armed
      Services Subcommittee on Readiness and Management Support Hearing
      on Contracting Issues in Iraq*, February 7, 2006, http://www.sigir.
      mil/files/testimony/SIGIR_Testimony_06-001T.pdf#view=fit;

Office of the Special Inspector General for Iraq Reconstruction (SIGIR), *Long-Standing Weaknesses in Department of State's Oversight of Dyncorp Contract for Support of the Iraqi Police Training Program*, January 25, 2010, http://www.sigir.mil/files/audits/10-008.pdf; Schorn, Daniel, "Billions Wasted In Iraq? U.S. Official Says Oversight Was 'Nonexistent,'" CBS News, February 12, 2006, http://www.cbsnews.com/stories/2006/02/09/60minutes/main1302378.shtml (accessed January 15, 2010).

88   IN 2001, RESPONDING TO THREATS U.S. Department of Defense, Office of the Assistant Secretary of Defense (Public Affairs), "Enduring Freedom Operational Update – Rear Adm. Stufflebeem," news release, Nov. 14, 2001, http://www.defense.gov/transcripts/transcript.aspx?transcriptid=2390.

88   THESE PACKAGES WERE THE SAME BBC, "Radio Warns Afghans Over Food Parcels," October 28, 2001, http://news.bbc.co.uk/2/hi/world/monitoring/media_reports/1624787.stm.

89   IN THIS CASE THE PACKAGES Elizabeth A. Neuffer, *Boston Globe*, "Report finds food airdrops in Afghanistan ineffective /Meal packs ruptured, spoiled – Were Mistaken for Bombs," *San Francisco Chronicle*, March 26, 2002, http://articles.sfgate.com/2002-03-26/news/17535206_1_aid-workers-humanitarian-daily-rations-airdrop.

89   Rosalind Russell, "Water Flows at Last in Southern Iraqi City," *ReliefWeb*, March 31, 2003, http://reliefweb.int/node/122616.

89   AS ONE EXAMPLE CBC, "Canada's Tsunami Response 'Amateur,' CARE Chief Says," February 3, 2005, http://www.cbc.ca/canada/story/2005/02/03/tsunami-care050203.html#ixzz1AwLh46oT.

89   FORMER CANADIAN PRIME MINISTER Paul Martin, *Hell or High Water: My Life In and Out of Politics* (Toronto: McClelland & Stewart, 2008), 346.

90 THE UNITED STATES, WHICH DEPLOYED Alex Dupuy,
"Commentary Beyond the Earthquake: A Wake-Up Call for
Haiti," *Latin American Perspectives* 37, no. 3, (May 2010): 199.

90 AFTER ASSUMING CONTROL OF THE AIRPORT Associated Press,
"Haiti Government Gets 1 cent of U.S. Aid Dollar," MSNBC,
January 27, 2010, http://www.msnbc.msn.com/id/35103622
/ns/world_news-haiti_earthquake/.

90 IN 1992, CANADA Dominic Leger and Nicolas Lemay-Hébert,
"Peacekeeping: A New Star," *Toronto Star*, May 29, 2010,
http://www.thestar.com/opinion/editorialopinion
/article/815587--peacekeeping-a-new-start.

90 TODAY IT IS SEVENTY-FIFTH United Nations, "Troop and Police
Contributors," March 31, 2018, https://peacekeeping.un.org
/en/troop-and-police-contributors.

91 THE UNITED STATES HAS FEWER Ibid.

91 THREE YEARS INTO THE CONFLICT *Telegraph*, "Deadly Attack
on Darfur Peacekeepers," July 10, 2008, http://www.telegraph.
co.uk/news/worldnews/africaandindianocean/sudan/2277834
/Deadly-attack-on-Darfur-peacekeepers.html.

91 IN 2007, THE AU/UN HYBRID OPERATION United Nations,
*Report of the Secretary-General on the Development of the African
Union–United Nations Hybrid Operation in Darfur*, UN Document
s/2007/653, November 5, 2007, 3.

91 WESTERN GOVERNMENTS WERE GENERALLY UNRESPONSIVE
Sudan Tribune, "Ethiopia to Provide 5 Tactical Helicopters to
Darfur Peacekeepers," April 9, 2009, http://www.sudantribune
.com/Ethiopia-to-provide-5-tactical,30825.

91 THE SAME DEFENCE DEPARTMENTS COULDN'T MUSTER
This is calculated based on United States military expenditures
in 2007 (when the helicopters were requested): $39.2 billion
in Afghanistan and $131.2 billion in Iraq, which totals

$170.4 billion in expenditures on both wars. The United Kingdom spent £7 billion ($14 billion) in Iraq and Afghanistan. Adding the U.S. and U.K.'s total military expenditures in Iraq and Afghanistan in 2007 and dividing it by 365 days equals $504 million per day. Amy Belasco, "The Cost of Iraq, Afghanistan, and Other Global Wars on Terror Operations Since 9/11," Congressional Research Service March 29, 2011, 7-5700 RL331102011, 3, http://www.fas.org/sgp/crs/natsec /RL33110.pdf.; Joseph Stiglitz and Linda Bilmes, "The Three Trillion Dollar War," *The Times*, February 23, 2008, http://www.timesonline.co.uk/tol/comment/columnists /guest_contributors/article3419840.ece.

92   AFTER THE 2005 EARTHQUAKE Tahir Andrabi and Jishnu Das, *In Aid We Trust: Hearts and Minds and the Pakistan Earthquake of 2005* (The World Bank Development Research Group Human Development and Public Services Team: October 1, 2010 Policy Research Working Paper 5440), http://econ.worldbank.org /external/default/main?entityID=000158349_20101005131809 &menuPK=64216926&pagePK=64165259&piPK=64165421&th eSitePK=469372.

92   BUT MILITARY-ADMINISTERED AID Greg Hansen, *Taking Sides or Saving Lives: Existential Choices for the Humanitarian Enterprise in Iraq* (Feinstein International Center: June 2007).

93   THE 1999 NATO MISSION Toby Porter, "The Partiality of Humanitarian Assistance – Kosovo in Comparative Perspective," *The Journal of Humanitarian Assistance*, June 17, 2000, http://jha.ac/2000/06/17/the-partiality-of-humanitarian - assistance-kosovo-in-comparative-perspective/.

93   THIS WAS DECRIED James Orbinski, *An Imperfect Offering: Humanitarian Action in the Twenty First Century* (Toronto: Anchor Canada, 2009).

93   AFRICOM's MANDATE U.S. Africa Command, "U.S. Africa
       Command Fact Sheet," September 2, 2010,
       http://www.africom.mil/AfricomFAQs.asp.

94   OVER THE PAST DECADE Aid Worker Society Security Database,
       Major Attacks on Aid Workers: Summary Statistics (2006-2016),
       https://aidworkersecurity.org/incidents/report/summary
       (accessed May 16, 2018).

94   THERE ARE NOW MORE AID WORKERS KILLED Ibid, 2.

94   IN IRAQ, THE BOMBING iCasualties, "Operation Iraqi
       Freedom," http://icasualties.org/Iraq/index.aspx
       (accessed May 21, 2011).

94   IN IRAQ, THE BOMBING Iraq Body Count, "Documented
       Civilian Deaths from Violence," accessed May 22, 2011,
       http://www.iraqbodycount.org/database.

95   MEANWHILE, SMALL ARMS FLOWED FREELY *USA Today*,
       "Saudis Reportedly Funding Iraq Sunni Insurgents,"
       December 8, 2006, http://www.usatoday.com/news/world
       /iraq/2006-12-08-saudis-sunnis_x.htm; Thomas Harding,
       "Iraqi Terrorists Are Being Supplied With Arms
       Smuggled from Iran," *Telegraph*, November 11, 2006,
       http://www.telegraph.co.uk/news/worldnews/middleeast
       /iraq/1533891/Iraqi-terrorists-are-being-supplied-with-arms
       -smuggled-from-Iran.html.

95   SHE HAD OFFERED Jason Burke, "Margaret Hassan, Relief
       Worker Who Dedicated Her Life to Helping the Iraqi People,"
       Guardian, November 17, 2004, http://www.guardian.co.uk
       /society/2004/nov/17/internationalaidanddevelopment.
       guardianobituaries.

95   EVEN THE MURDEROUS CREEP BBC, "'Zarqawi' Call to Release
       Hassan," November 6, 2004, http://news.bbc.co.uk/2/hi
       /middle_east/3987913.stm.

95 HER SISTERS ACCUSED BBC, "Sister in Plea over Hassan
Body," June 5, 2006, http://news.bbc.co.uk/2/hi/uk
_news/5047510.stm.

CHAPTER 4

100 DURING THE PREVIOUS SEVEN YEARS Terrence Lyons, "Liberia's
Path from Anarchy to Elections," Brookings, May 1, 1998,
previously published in *Current History* 97, no. 619 (May 1998):
229–233, http://www.brookings.edu/articles/1998/05africa
_lyons.aspx.

100 ACCORDING TO UNICEF Human Rights Watch, *Easy Prey:
Child Soldiers in Liberia* (Human Rights Watch: September 8,
1994), http://www.hrw.org/legacy/reports/1994/liberia2.

100 DURING THE NINETEENTH CENTURY Claude A. Clegg III,
*The Price of Liberty: African Americas and the Making of
Liberia* (Chapel Hill: The University of North Carolina
Press, 2004).

101 BY 1870, ALTHOUGH THESE IMMIGRANTS Morten Bøås,
"The Liberian Civil War: New War/Old War?" *Global Society:
Journal of Interdisciplinary International Relations* 19, no. 1,
(January 2005): 76.

101 FOR MORE THAN A CENTURY Ibid, 76.

101 "LURKING BENEATH THE SURFACE" Chris Hedges, *War Is a Force
That Gives Us Meaning*, (New York: Anchor Books, 2002), 45.

110 BY THE 1960s Peter Walker and Daniel Maxwell, *Shaping the
Humanitarian World* (New York: Routledge, 2009).

112 LESS THAN THREE WEEKS *The Chronicle of Philanthropy*,
"A Roundup of Haiti Fund Raising as of January 29," January
29, 2010, http://philanthropy.com/article/A-Roundup-of
-Haiti-Fund/63823.

114 BY COMPARISON, THE WAR International Rescue Committee, "IRC Study Shows Congo's Neglected Crisis Leaves 5.4 Million Dead; Peace Deal in N. Kivu, Increased Aid Critical to Reducing Death Toll," news release, January 22, 2008, http://www.rescue.org/news/irc-study-shows-congos -neglected-crisis-leaves-54-million-dead-peace-deal-n-kivu -increased-aid--4331.

114 Global Humanitarian Assistance, "Humanitarian Aid to Haiti, 1995–2010," http://www.globalhumanitarianassistance.org /countryprofile/haiti (accessed June 27, 2011); Global Humanitarian Assistance, "Humanitarian Aid to the Democratic Republic of Congo, 1995–2010," http://www.globalhumanitarianassistance.org /countryprofile/drc (accessed June 27, 2011); Global Humanitarian Assistance, "Total Humanitarian Aid to Sudan, 1995–2010," http://www.globalhumanitarianassistance.org /countryprofile/sudan (accessed June 27, 2011).

115 IT BECAME SO PROBLEMATIC Elizabeth Redman, "Call for Journalists in Haiti to Remain Objective, Keep Out of the Story," *The Editors Weblog*, January 25, 2010, http://www.editorsweblog.org/newsrooms_and_journalism /2010/01/call_for_journalists_in_haiti_to_remain.php.

118 Keith Tester, *Humanitarianism and Modern Culture* (University Park: Pennsylvania State University Press, 2010), 5.

119 BILL CLINTON WAS APPOINTED Jonathan M. Katz, "With Cheap Food Imports, Haiti Can't Feed Itself," *Huffington Post*, March 20, 2010, http://www.huffingtonpost.com/2010/03/20/ with-cheap-food-imports-h_n_507228.html.

123 IF AID IS STARTING World Vision, "2010 Annual Review," http://www.worldvision.org/content.nsf/about/ar-financials (accessed May 30, 2011).

124 THE LARGEST 1 PERCENT Imagine Canada, "Charities & Nonprofit Organizations," http://www.imaginecanada.ca /node/32 (accessed June 2, 2011).

124 WORLDWIDE, NGOs EMPLOY Kenneth Kidd, "Failure in 'the Republic of NGOs,'" *Toronto Star*, December 3, 2010, http://www.thestar.com/haiti/governance/article /901730--failure-in-the-republic-of-ngos.

125 WHILE THE FOCUS OF AID As evidence of this, the 2011 United Nations Sudan report is called "Beyond Emergency Relief: Longer-term Trends and Priorities for UN Agencies in Darfur," United Nations, September 2010, http://www.unsudanig.org /docs/Darfur_LT_100905_med.pdf.

125 BY THE END OF 2007 Richard Brennan, "Red Cross Yet to Spend $200M of Tsunami Cash," *Toronto Star*, March 3, 2008, http://www.thestar.com/News/Canada/article/308788.

CHAPTER 5

135 THE ENTIRE HUMANITARIAN MOVEMENT Ryszard Kapuscinski, *The Other*, trans. Antonia Lloyd-Jones (New York: Verso, 2008).

136 EFFORTS TO CURB SUCH PRACTICES UNICEF, *Principles and Guidelines for Ethical Reporting on Children and Young People under 18 Years Old*, http://www.unicef.org/eapro/Reporting_on _children_and_young_pp.pdf (accessed June 2, 2011); The Irish Association of Non Governmental Development Organisations, *Code of Conduct on Images and Messages* (2006), http://www.dochas.ie/Shared/Files/5/Images_and _Messages.pdf.

138 THE MEDIA HAVE KEENLY Laura Fitzpatrick, "Vacationing Like Brangelina," *Time*, July 26, 2007, http://www.time.com/time /magazine/article/0,9171,1647457,00.html.

139 VOLUNTOUR PROGRAMS, HOWEVER Gap Advice, "Gap Years in the Media," http://www.gapadvice.org/career-breaks /gap-years-in-the-media/(accessed May 30, 2011).

139 IN SOME CASES Ian Birrell, *Guardian*, "Before You Pay to Volunteer Abroad, Think of the Harm You Might Do," November 14, 2010, http://www.guardian.co.uk/commentis free/2010/nov/14/orphans-cambodia-aids-holidays-madonna.

140 THE BONDS THAT ARE FORMED Linda Richter and Amy Norman, "AIDS Orphan Tourism: A Threat to Young Children in Residential Care," *Vulnerable Children and Youth Studies* 5 no. 3, (2010), http:// qmul.academia.edu/AmyNorman/Papers/320707/AIDS_orphan_ tourism_A_threat_to_young_children_in_residential_care.

143 MORE THAN FORTY YEARS LATER Make Poverty History, "Reduce Global Poverty," http://www.makepovertyhistory.ca /learn/issues/reduce-global-poverty (accessed May 30, 2011).

143 IN 2016, DURING THE LARGEST OECD 2016 Data, *Net ODA*, https://data.oecd.org/oda/net-oda.htm (accessed September 22, 2017).

144 JOSEPH NYE, JR., HARVARD PROFESSOR Claire Provost, "U.S. Foreign Aid Takes Immediate Cuts, and Further Battles Loom," *Guardian*, April 14, 2011, http://www.guardian.co.uk /global-development/poverty-matters/2011/apr/14/us -foreign-aid-cuts-further-battles.

145 LOOKING BEYOND THE MALIGNANT David Koch, "Improving Child and Maternal Health Amidst Conflict in Afghanistan," UNICEF, http://www.unicef.org/infobycountry/afghanista _ 47807.html (accessed May 30, 2011).

147 IT WAS . . . AN EASY CRIME Claudia Rosett, "Oil, Food and a Whole Lot of Questions," *New York Times*, April 18, 2003, http://www.nytimes.com/2003/04/18/opinion/oil-food -and-a-whole-lot-of-questions.html?pagewanted=2&src=pm.

147 THE REST WAS SPENT United Nations' Office of the Iraq Programme, "Oil-for-Food in Brief," November 23, 2003, http://www.un.org/Depts/oip/background/inbrief.html.

148 BY THE TIME THE PROGRAM WAS AXED United Nations, "The United Nations Is Extremely Concerned About the Serious Allegations of Corruption Surrounding the Oil-for-Food Programme," http://www.un.org/News/dh/iraq/oip /facts-oilforfood.htm (accessed May 30, 2011).

148 EVENTUALLY, AN EIGHTEEN-MONTH Claudia Rosett, "Annan's Son Took Payments Through 2004," *New York Sun*, November 26, 2004, http://www.nysun.com/foreign/annans-son-took -payments-through-2004/5372/.

150 THE LOSS OF HUNDREDS OF THOUSANDS Jamie N. Slotterback, "Threadbare: The Used Clothing Trade and Its Effects on the Textile Industries in Nigeria and Other Subsaharan African Nations," *Contemporary Perspectives* (seminar paper prepared for Dr. Tom Schrand, November 2007), http://www.philau.edu /schools/liberalarts/news/documents/SlotterbackSET.pdf.

153 NGOs DON'T HAVE TO BE BIG Ploughshares Fund, http://www.ploughshares.org (accessed May 30, 2011).

153 BUT THESE KINDS OF ORGANIZATIONS Al Norman, "Wal-Mart Gun Policy Courts Big City Mayors," *Huffington Post*, April 14, 2008, http://www.huffingtonpost.com/al-norman/wal-mart -gun-policy-court_b_96674.html.

CHAPTER 6

164 BASED ON A LANDMARK STUDY Emmanuela Gakidou et al., "Increased Educational Attainment and Its Effect on Child Mortality in 175 Countries Between 1970 and 2009: A Systematic Analysis," *The Lancet* 376 (September 2010): 959–974.

168 IN A CLIMATE WHERE WOMEN While women are legally entitled to inherit and own land in Afghanistan, this rarely occurs. According to the Afghanistan-based Women and Children Legal Research Foundation (WCLRF), "in practice women have very little access to property and control over their own income and properties." Mary Slosson, "UNIFEM Announces New Grants to Empower Women Across the Globe," *MediaGlobal*, January 18, 2010, http://www.mediaglobal.org /article/2010-01-21/unifem-announces-new-grants-to -empower-women-across-the-globe.

170 THEY BEGIN REACTING TO EXTERNAL Incite! Women of Color Against Violence, ed., *The Revolution Will Not be Funded: Beyond the Non-profit Industrial Complex* (Cambridge: South End Press, 2007).

171 THE WOMEN'S MOVEMENT IN LIBERIA David Smith, "Ivory Coast Women Defiant After Being Targeted by Gbagbo's Guns," *Guardian*, March 11, 2011, http://www.guardian.co.uk /world/2011/mar/11/ivory-coast-women-defiant.

172 THE WOMEN WERE AGGRESSIVELY CONFRONTED *Christian Science Monitor*, "In Egypt's Tahrir Square, Women Attacked at Rally on International Women's Day," , http://www.csmonitor .com/World/Middle-East/2011/0308/In-Egypt-s-Tahrir-Square -women-attacked-at-rally-on-International-Women-s-Day/(page) (accessed May 23, 2011).

172 THE WOMEN WERE PROTESTING Sheema Khan, "Egypt's Revolution Is Leaving Women Behind," *Globe and Mail*, April 7, 2011, http://www.theglobeandmail.com/news/opinions /opinion/egypts-revolution-is-leaving-women-behind /article1973918.

172 THEY WERE SHOUTED DOWN Ibid.

172 SOME BOLDLY MARCHED *Huffington Post*, "Ivory Coast Forces Kill 6 Women in Protest," March 3, 2011, http://www.huffingtonpost.com/2011/03/03/forces-kill -6-women-march_n_830857.html.

173 AMONG THE TWENTY-FIVE COUNTRIES Richard P. Cincotta and Elizabeth Leahy, "Population Age Structure and Its Relation to Civil Conflict: A Graphic Metric," *Environmental Change and Security Program Report* 12 (March 2007): 55, http://www.humansecuritygateway.com/documents /WILSON_PopulationAgeStructure_CivilConflict.pdf.

175 "CITIZENS VICTIMIZED BY GENOCIDE" Samantha Power, *A Problem from Hell: America and the Age of Genocide* (New York: Basic Books, 2002), 515.

176 MORE RECENT RESEARCH Scott Atran, "Trends in Suicide Terrorism: Sense and Nonsense," Presented to World Federation of Scientists Permanent Monitoring Panel on Terrorism, Erice, Sicily, August 2004, http://sitemaker.umich.edu/satran/files /atran-trends.pdf; Fathali M. Moghaddam, "The Staircase to Terrorism: A Psychological Exploration," *American Psychologist* 60, no. 2 (February–March 2005): 161–69; Rebecca L. Collins, "For Better or For Worse: The Impact of Upward Social Comparison on Self-evaluations," *Psychological Bulletin* 116, no. 1 (1996): 51–69; Serge Guimond and Lise Dubé-Simard, "Relative Deprivation Theory and The Quebec Nationalist Movement: The Cognition-Emotion Distinction and The Person-Group Deprivation and Issue," *Journal of Personality and Social Psychology* 44, no. 3 (1983): 526–35; Joanne Martin, Philip Brickman, and Alan Murray, "Moral Outrage and Pragmatism: Explanations for Collective Action," *Journal of Experimental Social Psychology* 20, no. 5 (September 1984): 484–496.

176 WHILE IMPROVING EDUCATIONAL LEVELS Christine Fair, ed.,
    Suicide Attacks in Afghanistan (2001–2007) (United Nations
    Assistance Mission in Afghanistan, September 2007), 29,
    http://home.comcast.net/~christine_fair/pubs/suicide
    _attacks_UNAMA.pdf; Christina Paxson, "Comment on
    Alan Krueger and Jitka Maleckova, 'Education, Poverty, and
    Terrorism: Is There a Causal Connection?'" (Princeton:
    Research Program in Development Studies, May 8 2002).

176 WOULD THERE HAVE BEEN ANY NEED *Guardian,*
    "EU Arms Exports to Libya: Who Armed Gaddafi?"
    http://www.guardian.co.uk/news/datablog/2011/mar/01
    /eu-arms-exports-libya (accessed May 19, 2011).

176 David Leigh and John Hooper, "Britain's Dirty Secret,"
    Guardian, March 6, 2003, http://www.guardian.co.uk
    /politics/2003/mar/06/uk.iraq.

180 ENDORSED BY WORLD LEADERS International Coalition for the
    Responsibility to Protect, www.responsibilitytoprotect.org.

187 IT IS TIME THEY HEARD FROM YOU Raise Hope for
    Congo, "Conflict Minerals Company Rankings,"
    http://www.raisehopeforcongo.org/content/conflict
    -minerals-company-rankings (accessed May 30, 2011).

187 THE WAR IN DARFUR UNICEF, "Darfur – overview,"
    http://www.unicef.org/infobycountry/sudan_darfur
    overview.html (accessed May 19, 2011).

189 AND LIKE MORE THAN HALF UNICEF, "Sudan: Background,"
    http://www.unicef.org/infobycountry/sudan_background
    .html (accessed May 22, 2011).

INDEX

SAMANTHA NUTT, M.D., is an award-winning humanitarian, acclaimed public speaker, and a leading authority on the impact of war on civilians. As founder and executive director of the internationally renowned organizations War Child Canada and War Child U.S.A., Dr. Nutt has worked with children and their families at the frontline of many of the world's major crises — from Iraq to Afghanistan, Somalia to the Democratic Republic of Congo, and Sierra Leone to Darfur, Sudan.

As one of the most original and influential voices in the humanitarian arena, Dr. Nutt is a respected authority for many of North America's leading media outlets. Her TED Talk on the deadly impact of small arms garnered over one million views on TED.com. Dr. Nutt has been appointed to the Order of Canada, Canada's highest civilian honour, for her contributions to improving the plight of young people in the world's worst conflict zones.

Dr. Nutt is a staff physician at Women's College Hospital in Toronto and an assistant professor of medicine at the University of Toronto. She is on the board of the David Suzuki Foundation. Dr. Nutt currently resides in Toronto with her husband and their son.